FIVE YEARS IN AMERICA

The Menominee Collection of Antoine Marie Gachet

PRO ETHNOGRAPHI©A COLLECTIONS

Volume 1   Series Editor: François Ruegg

FIVE YEARS IN AMERICA

The Menominee Collection of Antoine Marie Gachet

Sylvia S. Kasprycki

with a contribution by Anton Rotzetter

Series editor: François Ruegg

Pro Ethnographi©a
Fribourg, Suisse

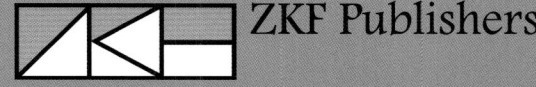 ZKF Publishers

Five Years in America. The Menominee Collection of Antoine Marie Gachet / Sylvia S. Kasprycki,
with a contribution by Anton Rotzetter and an introduction by François Ruegg.
Altenstadt 2018: ZKF Publishers
        Includes bibliographic references.
        ISBN 978-3-9811620-9-7 (ZKF Publishers)
        ISBN 978-2-9701063-1-9 (Pro Ethnographi©a)

Bibliographical Information
The Deutsche Bibliothek lists this publication in the German National Bibliography; detailed bib-
liographic data are available in the internet at http://dnb.ddb.de

Distributed by
The University of Oklahoma Press
Norman, Oklahoma
oupress.com

Graphic design: Sylvia S. Kasprycki
Image editing: Christian Feest

Cover illustrations:
        Detail of beaded mittens (Gachet collection, cat.no. 2001)
        Detail of decorated pipestem (Gachet collection, cat.no. 2055)

Printed and bound in Austria (European Union)
by Ferdinand Berger & Söhne GmbH, Horn

CONTENTS

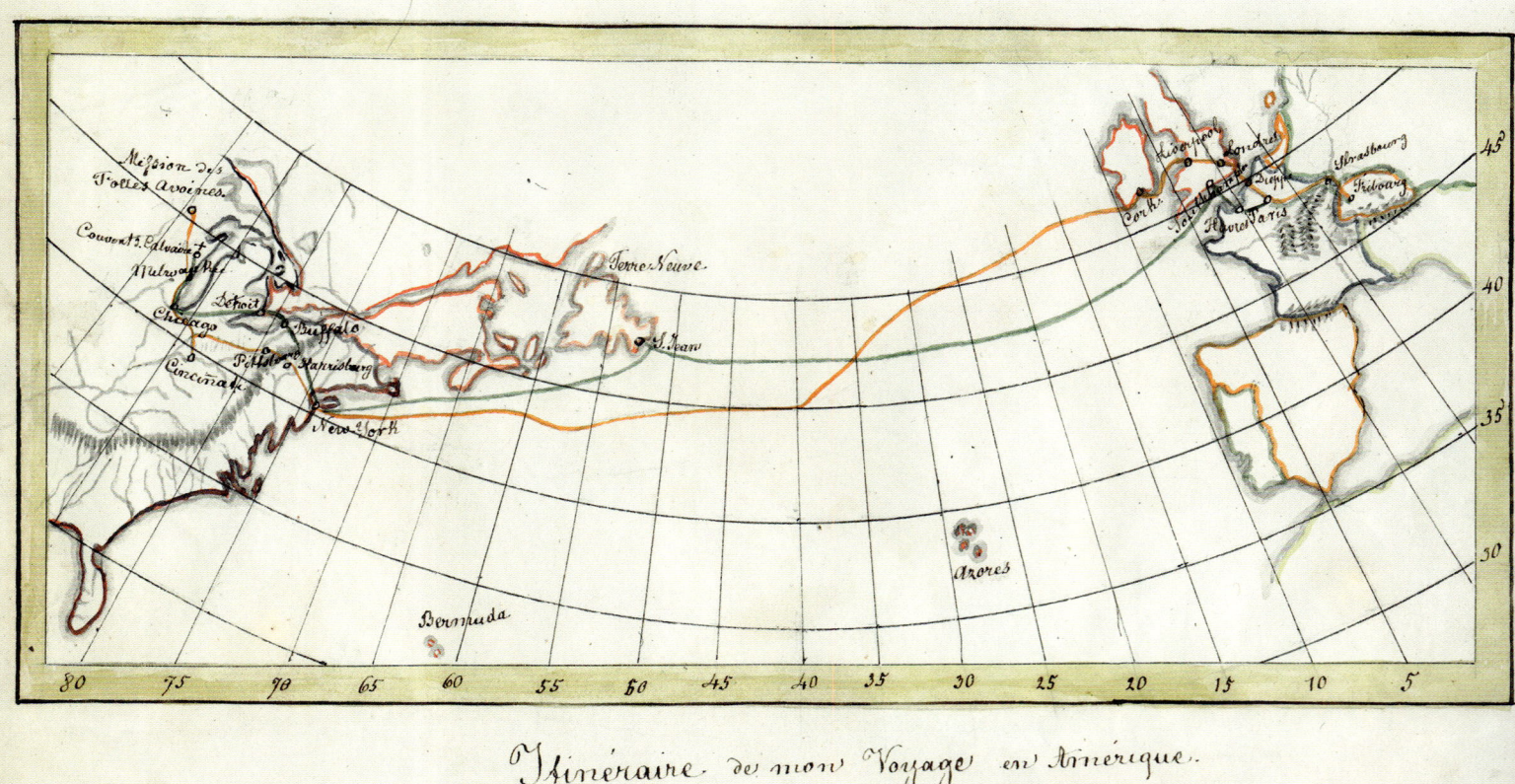

Fig. 1
Itinerary of My Travels in America. Outward journey in blue, return in red.
Drawing by Antoine Marie Gachet ("American Diary," p. 261). Courtesy of the Capuchin Friary, Fribourg.

PREFACE

Since 2013 the Association Pro Ethnographi©a directed by Professor François Ruegg has devoted itself to the preservation of the ethnographic collections belonging to the patrimony of Fribourg. The Association has committed itself to safeguard and catalogue the collections, encompassing about 2,500 objects, originally held by the Department of Social Anthropology of the University of Fribourg and assembled by Antoine Marie Gachet, OFM Cap, Wilhelm Koppers, SVD, Georg Höltker, SVD, and others. This effort is aimed at rescuing these documents of cultural diversity, mainly dating from the nineteenth and twentieth centuries, from oblivion and making them available to scholarship and to an interested public. Fribourg has always had its share of explorers who went abroad in search of the Other. Their voyages have resulted in friendships, exchanges, and gifts forming the basis of collections preserving a historical record of foreign cultures, many of which have undergone dramatic changes in the process of globalization.

The present book focuses on the work of Antoine Marie Gachet, a nineteenth-century missionary from Fribourg, among the Menominees, a Native American nation in Wisconsin. It is the fruit of many years of research by Dr. Sylvia Kasprycki on the unique contribution of Father Gachet to the historical ethnography of the Menominees. This catalogue, enriched with photographs by the Fribourg artist Francesco Ragusa, endeavors to create a permanent monument to a facet of the history of Fribourg—that of our explorers.

Marie Garnier
State Councilor, Fribourg

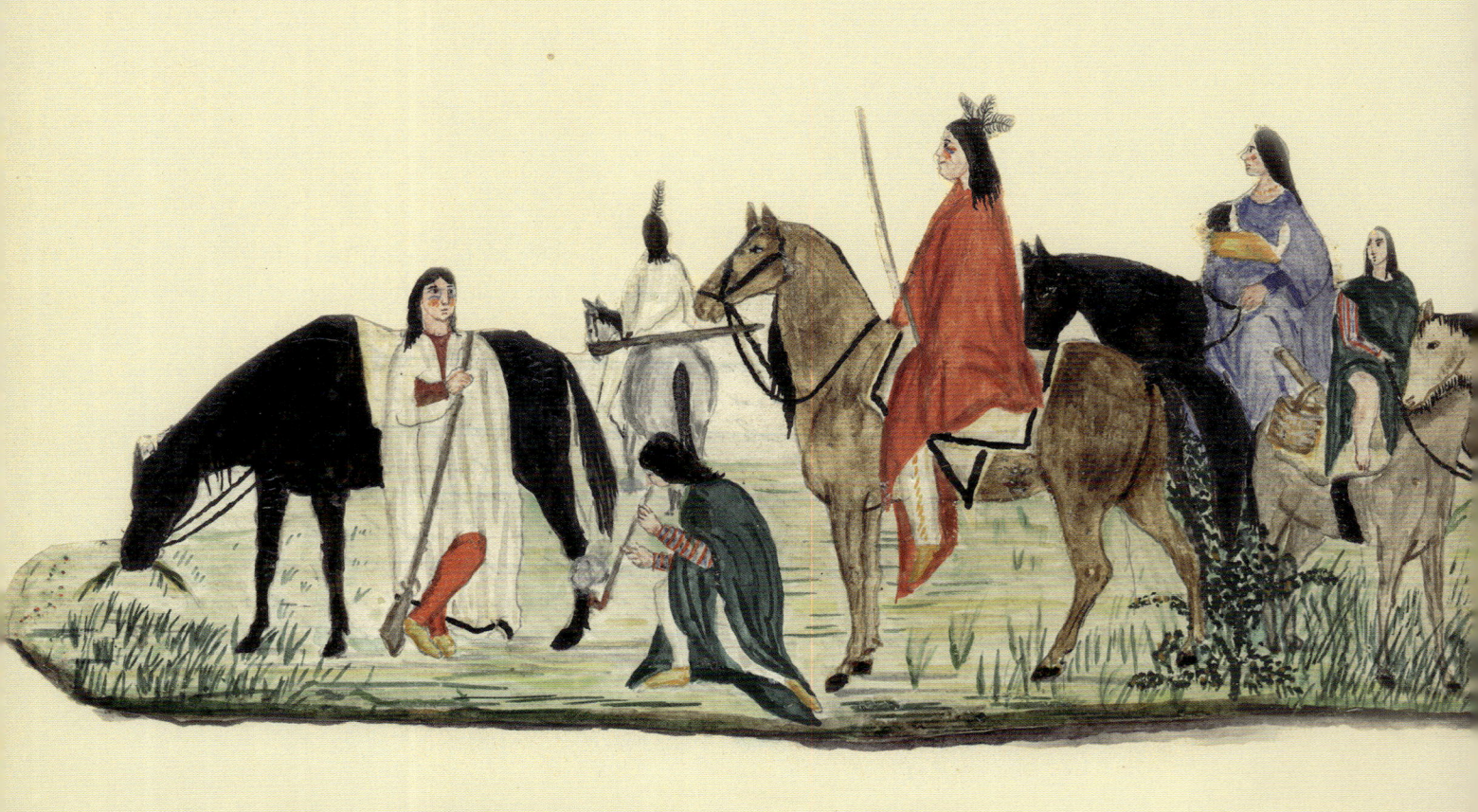

EDITOR'S INTRODUCTION
The Gachet Collection in Fribourg:
A Precious Link in a Long Chain

François Ruegg

Fig. 2
Indians Traveling.
Drawing by Antoine Marie Gachet ("American Diary," p. 276). Courtesy of the Capuchin Friary, Fribourg.

Although today composed of less than thirty objects, the Gachet collection in Fribourg, Switzerland, bears witness to the rich cultural heritage of the Menominees, one of the Indian societies living in Wisconsin. The personality of its collector, the Capuchin Father Antoine Marie Gachet (1822–1890), a citizen of Gruyères in the Canton of Fribourg, adds a special dimension to this collection. Gachet was more than just a missionary. He became interested in the Menominees' culture and pursued linguistic and ethnographic studies about "his" congregation. He also wrote a diary, already at that time following a professional anthropologist's methodology![1]

Father Gachet is one of the many Catholic missionaries who, after having severely judged the "pagans" they wanted to convert, eventually became charmed by many of their human qualities and started collecting the handicrafts they produced. Surely Gachet's ultimate goal was that of bringing these "poor souls" away from their "dark devilish superstitions" to the light of Christianity or, more precisely, to the bosom of the Catholic Church. However, at the same time he compiled precious testimonies of their daily ways of life both in writing in his journal and in assembling a collection of objects that is now finally presented as a whole and published in a systematic catalogue herewith.

The recent history of this dormant collection may appear awkward to the reader. Objects being "exhumed" and lent from time to time to international exhibitions on Native American ethnography in Europe were the only sign posts to the lay anthropologist that I am in this field that pointed to the value of the hidden treasure we had concealed in the basement of the Institute of Social Anthropology of the University of Fribourg, where I have been teaching for the last fifteen years. As a matter of fact, the Institute has for many years been

[1] Gachet's diary, interspersed with scholarly reflections, was published as *Cinq ans en Amérique: Journal d'un missionnaire* (Gachet 1890).

the curator—or rather the guardian—of several collections and scattered ethnographic objects from all over the world, except for the regions its professors and researchers were working on! The main focus of the Chair is rather the south and the east of Europe, particularly postsocialist societies.

With the exception of Gachet's collection, the ethnographic collections were actually acquired by former professors at the Institute, notably Wilhelm Koppers (1886–1961), who carried out fieldwork in India, and Georg Höltker (1895–1976) in Papua New Guinea. The latter have nevertheless one point in common with Gachet: they all were missionaries. The Chair of the *Seminar für Anthropologie* was until 1989 filled by professors belonging to the missionary order of the Society of the Divine Word (SVD), who specialized in African, Oceanian, or Indian ethnography (see Ruegg 2015). Under the banner of their founding father, the famous anthropologist Wilhelm Schmidt (1868–1954), also founder, with Koppers, of the so-called Vienna School of Anthropology, they pursued their difficult task: that of conjugating a scientific vocation with a religious one. It was for Wilhelm Schmidt that the Canton of Fribourg opened a Chair for Ethnology in 1942; Schmidt was also the director of the Vatican's *Museo Missionario Etnologico* from 1926 to 1939.[2]

However, in 1962 the Fribourg branch of the SVD, its library, most part of its ethnographic collections, as well as the editorial office of the scientific journal *Anthropos* moved to newly built facilities in St. Augustin near Bonn. Since then only little has been done to value the collections remaining in Fribourg. They were stored in cardboard boxes in a basement, partially inventoried, and visited only occasionally by specialists. Other ethnographic objects have been donated by travelers or amateurs. Students have also been involved, mainly in the dusting of the boxes! A first grant from the University allowed us to establish a state of the art on the collections and on Pater Schmidt's activities in Fribourg.

In 2013 the association Pro Ethnographi©a was created in order to digitize the objects, complete the hand- or machine-written dusty catalogues, and bring them out of oblivion. Pro Ethnographi©a's aims are: 1. to ensure the conservation and digitization of the collections as well as make them accessible to researchers; 2. to make social anthropology (ethnology) known to an informed public, in both academic and ludic approaches, through the use of objects, image, and text; 3. to further research the history of the Fribourg collections and their initiators in the broader context of missionary anthropology and its scientific contribution to the field.

Non-profit, apolitical, and non-confessional in its nature, Pro Ethnographi©a is not intended to build up a museum nor to display the objects for the general public. It works with any private or public institution, foundation, research institute, museum, or individual who shares its objectives. Its projects are temporary and aim to be flexible. The collections are not linked to any specific geographical place, aside from their provenance, i.e., the University of Fribourg. After

[2] Thanks to the intervention of Pope Pius XI, Schmidt had been able to leave Vienna (where he was under house arrest by the Gestapo) for Rome in 1938, before moving to Fribourg the same year. For a detailed account of his odyssey from Vienna to Fribourg and on the creation of the Vatican museum, see Rohrbacher 2012.

negotiations with the Rector of the University, the collections are now owned by Pro Ethnographi©a. They were transferred in 2015 to a safer home in the Château de Bulle, thanks to the welcome of the local and cantonal authorities.

In reading Gachet's diary, I was particularly struck by the mixed populations he met in Wisconsin at his time. Truth be told, I still had a naive idea of the "wilderness" that missionaries like him went into. Indeed, the fact that German, Irish, Yankee—as he calls them—and even Swiss colonists where already settled in the region gives this great epic a different tone. Gachet was operating in an already globalized world, where Indians had been exposed to and influenced by the other settlers, as some of their artifacts show, such as the boxes in which the maple cardies were stored. The maple syrup industry is perhaps one of the best examples of successful Native adaptation to new economic challenges. In this sense, the ethnographic record left by Gachet also reflects the history of cultural interaction and the creative strategies by Native peoples in the face of often destructive acculturation pressures.

It has certainly been a great pleasure to benefit from the precious collaboration with an expert, Dr. Sylvia Kasprycki, in the realization of this catalogue raisonné. Author of many books and articles on the Menominees and their culture, she has also tackled the difficult question of missionary ethnography. This is particularly interesting in our case, since, as aforementioned, the majority of our collections are linked with ethnographers who were also missionaries. Our hope is that all scholars involved in missionary ethnography will exchange knowledge and experience and, who knows, even build a network that will allow for a better overview of this particular aspect of ethnography.

The late Professor Anton Rotzetter, from the Capuchin Order in Fribourg, kindly consented to contribute a chapter on Gachet's biography and activities in India. He has also been instrumental in making accessible Gachet's original drawings, resurfaced after more than a century. Permission by the Capuchin Friary of Fribourg to publish a substantial selection of these images alongside the Menominee artifacts which constitute the collection is herewith gratefully acknowledged.

We co hope that this new publication will contribute to the knowledge of North American Indians as well as underline the valuable contribution of the collector and scholar Gachet, one of the many forefathers of our discipline.

Without the precious and constant support of the Le Cèdre Foundation and the contribution of Le Cercle fribourgeois, this project would not have been possible. It is with profound gratitude that I am mentioning their philanthropic purposes.

Fribourg, June 2018
Prof. emeritus Dr. François Ruegg
President of Pro Ethnographi©a
Chair of Social Anthropology,
University of Fribourg (Switzerland)

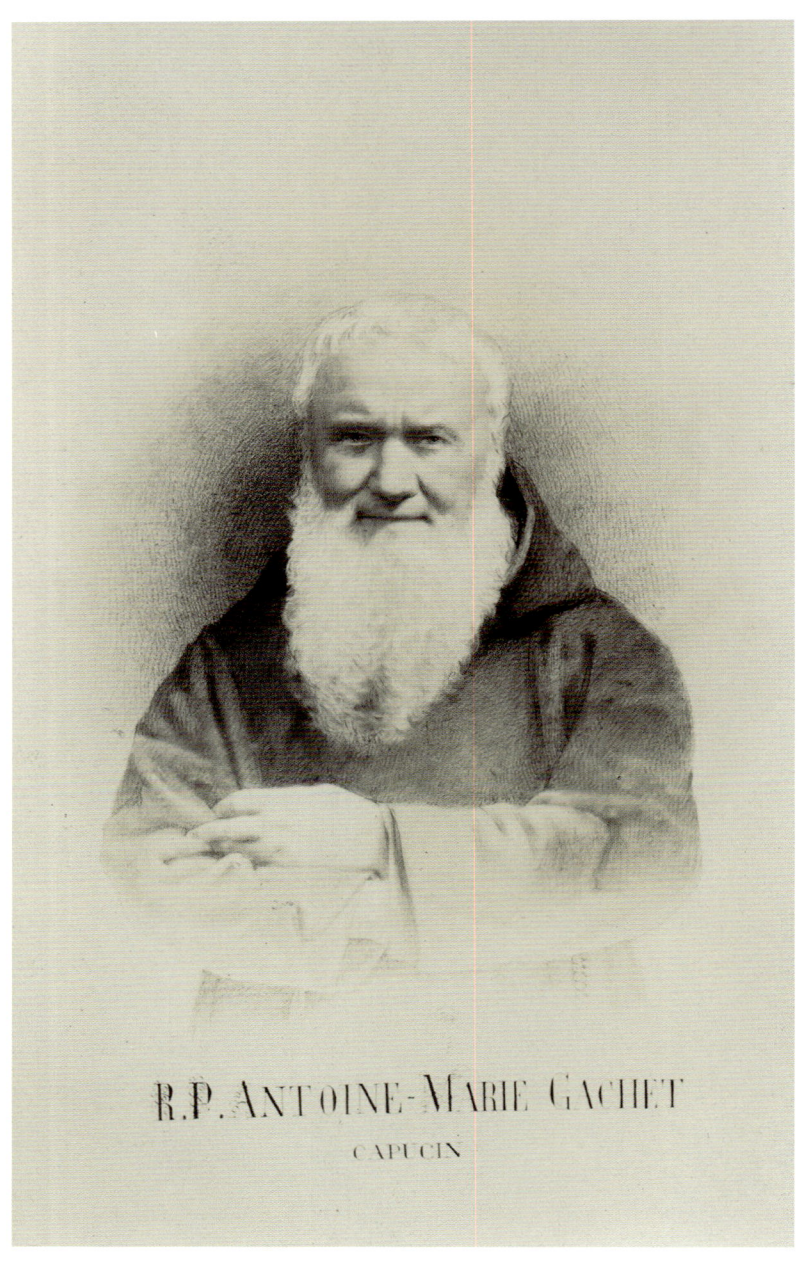

R.P. ANTOINE-MARIE GACHET

CAPUCIN

Fig. 3
Antoine Marie Gachet, OFM Cap (1822–1890) in his late years.
Undated cabinet photograph, Studio Ernest Lorson, Fribourg. Courtesy of the
Capuchin Friary, Fribourg.

INTEREST AS VOCATION
On the Biography of the Capuchin Antoine Marie Gachet (1822–1890)

Anton Rotzetter

Before presenting the biography[1] of Antoine Marie Gachet, I would like to highlight the spiritual horizon within which he shaped his life.

In the Franciscan Tradition

The Capuchins, of whom Gachet was a member, are a branch of the Order of St. Francis. Its founder, Francis of Assisi (1182–1226), was the first founder of an order to include a "chapter on missions" into his rules.[2] This, however, is an anachronism because Francis was not primarily interested in the dogmatic diffusion of Christianity, as it would be the case in the course of subsequent centuries.[3] The title later added to this chapter 16 reads: "Of those who want to go among the Saracens [inter Saracenos] or other infidels." The text itself refers to two forms of spiritual presence among them [inter eos]. One form is "not to engage in arguments or disputes but to be subject to every human creature for God's sake and to acknowledge that they are Christians" (Francis of Assisi 1999: 74; cp. Berg and Lehmann 2009: 81f.). What needs to be underlined here is the subservience required of the Brothers in their cohabitation with people of another culture. This attitude, however, applies in principle to social conditions among Christians as well. The Brothers should always consider themselves as "inter-ested," as such that are "in between," amidst the lepers and the poor, among humans in general. This inter-est is a precondition for what is called interest in the narrow sense of the word and what is associated with a certain curiosity about the Other. The second form of Franciscan presence is the call for conversion. But once again this does not mean dogmatic proselytization but the laical discourse of the necessity of the recognition of God and Jesus Christ (Rotzetter 1982).

[1] Here I would like to express my gratitude to my confrère Fidelis Stöckli for making available to me the data base on Bishop Anastasius Hartmann. The result of this laborious work has become an excellent working tool.

[2] "Regula non bullata" (Esser 1978: 268f).

[3] I have interpreted this chapter on several occasions, i.a., Rotzetter 1984, 1994, 2008.

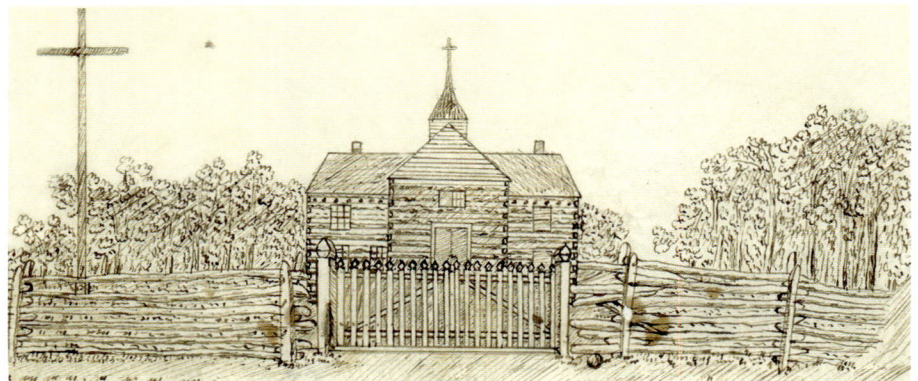

Fig. 4
Church of Calvary.
Drawing by Antoine Marie
Gachet ("American Diary,"
p. 25). Courtesy of the
Capuchin Friary, Fribourg.

Integral to this Franciscan horizon is the "religious obedience," according to which someone must not conduct one's life in an individualistic manner. What is more important is to fit oneself into a greater whole and to pursue goals which are by and large defined by the order. Gachet's biography illustrates at various points of intersection what obedience actually means. The extent to which he was able to feel guilty and to be ready to carry the consequences of transgressions is shown by his letter to Bishop Anastasius Hartmann (MA IV: 354–361), who for a short period of time was procurator of missions and as such also his superior. Hartmann had demanded his absolute obedience: Gachet had no other assignment than to secure the newly founded friary of Mt. Calvary (cp. Schweizer 2007) as guardian and master of novices, and he was therefore not permitted to leave it in order to live among the Menominees (MA IV: 343f.). This letter reached Gachet only after he had already left Mt. Calvary. In his reply he not only expressed his remorse but also outlined the "sad situation" of the friary, which in the meantime had become untenable and unbearable to him. His decision to work as a missionary among the Menominees had been reached after conversations with a confrère and with the consent of the responsible Bishop of Milwaukee, Johann Martin Henni.[4] With his action he also wanted to provoke an intervention on the part of Rome. Here we can recognize the dialogical understanding of Franciscan obedience (Rotzetter 1977: 130–140; 2013: 69–100), to which Gachet was committed for all of his life.

Life in Fribourg

Antoine Marie Gachet was born on 8 April 1822 in the city of Fribourg (Freiburg) in Switzerland.[5] His parental home was in the lower city,[6] he was baptized in the cathedral, and he received the first communion. He went to school in Fribourg, attended the Jesuit "Gymnasium" St. Michael, and in 1841 entered into the noviciate of the Capuchins. In 1846 he was ordained to the priesthood and subsequently served from Fribourg as priest and preacher in many parishes

[4] To him Anastasius Hartmann had also written a German letter demanding Gachet's obedience (MA IV: 345). The name of the bishop is variously spelled in the sources.
  It is interesting to note in this context that the Minister General of the order, Maurus of Perugia, in a letter of September 1861 expresses his joy about the progress of Gachet's work among the Menominees. At the same time he gives him permission to keep the cow Gachet had bought (MA IV: 666).

[5] Not in Gruyères (Greyerz), as has been asserted time and again in the wake of Blaise Favre, who in turn took this information from an obituary (see below). Gruyères was Gachet's place of citizenship but not his birthplace. This difference is a Swiss peculiarity.

[6] All these autobiographical data were reported by him in his "Asian Diary" (MA V: 813).

of the canton Fribourg. From 1853 to 1855 he was guardian (the Capuchin term for the house superior) of the friary in Fribourg as well as novice master. Thus, he assumed the same functions held two years before his entering the order by Anastasius Hartmann. Gachet certainly recognized the disciplinary and ambient reforms implemented by the latter in the Fribourg friary (cp. Gachet 1876: 11f.; Hartmann 2003: 43f.). In order to prepare himself for his missionary activities he studied—somewhat surprisingly—Hebrew with the later Bishop of Fribourg, Christophore Cosandey.[7] But for the same purpose and more to the point, he pursued studies of English and other subjects at the College St. Fidelis of Sigmaringen in Rome.

Gachet remained a Fribourgeois all of his life. Time and again he remembers the city of his birth in his diaries, time and again he compares what he observes with the conditions in his native Fribourg.

Interest among the Menominees

The actual reason for A. M. Gachet's departure for Wisconsin in November 1857 was at first only indirectly related to missionary work. He was supposed to head, as guardian und novice master, the Capuchin friary of Mt. Calvary that had been founded by the two secular priests Gregor Haas (subsequently P. Bonaventura) and Johann Frey (later P. Franz). But as has already been related, it took only one year and a half for Gachet to withdraw himself from the tensions developing in the friary. His own contribution to this situation became apparent from a historical retrospective prepared in 1907 by the now considerably grown province (MA IV: 361f.). According to this account, the alienation had also been caused by Gachet's absence of up to three days per week because of pastoral responsibilities.

A. M. Gachet was an interested observer of his environment. He had the extraordinary ability to describe and draw what he had seen in great detail and in epic broadness. The richly illustrated original manuscripts based on his diaries preserved in the Capuchin friary in Fribourg are true treasures and irreplaceable sources, especially also for ethnography.[8] As far as the Menominees are concerned, they have been and will be appreciated in this volume from an expert point of view (cp. Kasprycki 2005, 2006). From the viewpoint of religious studies, the Capuchin Blaise Favre (1954a) has summarized his findings in his unpublished licence thesis. He sees Gachet as describing the religious trajectory of the Menominees as a spiritualization of totemism. To the same author we are indebted for a work on Gachet's Menominee grammar (Favre 1954b). In view of the extremely short period of his sojourn among this people, one can recognize his ingenious sense for grammatical structures. From a scholarly point of view it may therefore be regrettable that his time in America was abruptly terminated.

[7] For this and the following details, see Grangier 1891.

[8] Contrary to the information available to Kasprycki (2006: 49), the manuscripts Gachet prepared for publication have neither perished nor disappeared.

Volume 1, the "American Diary" (Cinq ans en Amérique, 1857–1862) was first published in a series of newspaper articles in the Revue de la Suisse catholique and subsequently also in book form (Gachet 1890). A second, undated version is also preserved in the archive of the Fribourg friary; a handwritten slip of paper notes that the two editions are not totally concordant and that after Gachet's death the editor of the journal also wanted to publish volume 2, a plan aborted after only two instalments.

Volume 2, the "Asian Diary" (Cinq ans en Asie, Indes orientales 1863–1868), was eventually published in MA V: 797–1174. For the aborted initial publication see Revue de la Suisse catholique 1890: 912; 1891: 37.

Both manuscript diaries are richly illustrated with colored drawings, which had not been included in the publication of the "American Diary."

Interest in India

In May 1862 A. M. Gachet was ordered to go to India to assist the aging Bishop Anastasius Hartmann. For him this meant relocating into a completely different world. Whereas he ultimately passed a positive judgement on the cultural and religious world of the Menominees, he persisted in his negative assessment of the religions of India, which is already spelled out in his American diary. While acknowledging the gradual approximation to "theism" of the former, he sees the latter as the "worst form of idolatry" (MA V: 797).[9] At the time of his departure from India in 1868, his pronouncements still sound very similar. He views the whole continent as "Satan's sovereign territory," where "one finds so many obvious traces of his infernal despotism." In spite of this he sings India's praise because it was here that he received the gift of an encounter with a saint, Anastasius Hartmann, whose life he described in German, French, and English (MA V: 1111, 1095). He speaks of the "terrible secret of Brahmanism," of the "sacrilege of Buddhism," and he calls out to both of them: "When will you cease to poison this country?" In the same passage he also curses Protestantism (MA V: 1112). The blessing of a tree by a Hindu priest he calls a "malédiction," and the priests themselves "functionaries of the devil" (MA V: 1054).

Although Gachet could indeed also be affected by the seriousness of the fasting and prayers of Muslims (MA V: 885, 897) or of a Hindu girl, this affection was muted by the regret that they were not baptized and thus were forfeiting eternal salvation. "At the same time I was filled with bitter thoughts about the fate of this child, who has so wonderfully been created for prayer, with a soul that is 'naturaliter christiana' [Christian by nature]" (MA V: 1054). Here there is a flash of an idea that would have permitted a different theological evaluation. Gachet always describes feasts, rites, and other phenomena from a certain theological remove. Thus, e.g., he draws at great length a negative image of the fakir (frightening, disgusting, extreme, staged holiness, craving for compassion; MA V: 989) and reaches a harsh verdict: "More and more European civilization is putting its stamp on the various regions of India. But this is merely a material and intellectual progress, whereas the most noble parts of the soul remain unaffected by it. The educated Hindu is as bad, as immoral after the metamorphosis as before it. Previously he was an immoral idolater, now he is a deist, an elegant pantheist, or more often an immoral atheist. Then why should a deist, pantheist, or atheist care for morals? He shows morality as long as customs or external relations demand it. But beyond that all morals come to an end. You will find educated Hindus who are like Europeans, yet infidels. The time will come when the Catholic missionary will no longer exclusively have to make an attempt to convert the idolaters, but to convert the infidels of black or brown complexion, just as in the cities of Europe" (MA V: 1074f.). His verdict on Islam does not

[9] Translations from the French by Anton Rotzetter.

[10] Singhalese: MA V: 908; fur traders: MA V: 1001; nomadic "bohémiens": MA V: 1001; Brahmans, Muslims, Nepalese, Buddhists, castes: Gachet 1876: 19 and MA V: 924.

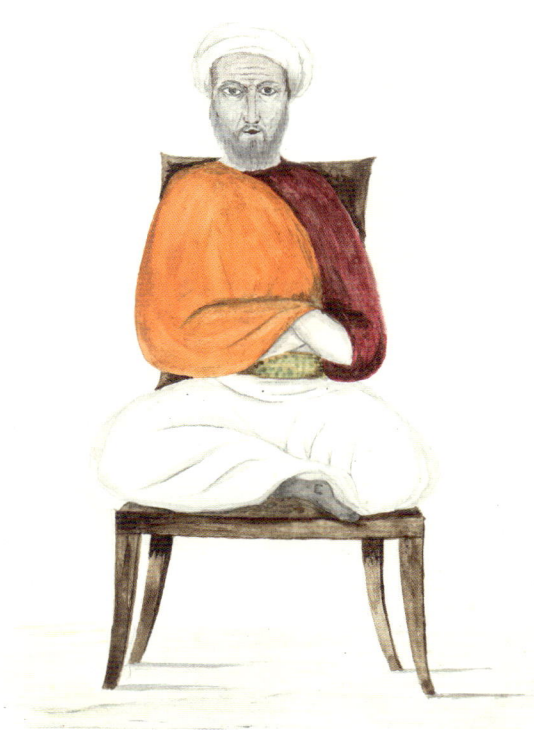

Fig. 5
[Man from Patna, India].
Drawing by Antoine Marie Gachet ("Asian Diary," p. 5).
Courtesy of the Capuchin Friary, Fribourg.

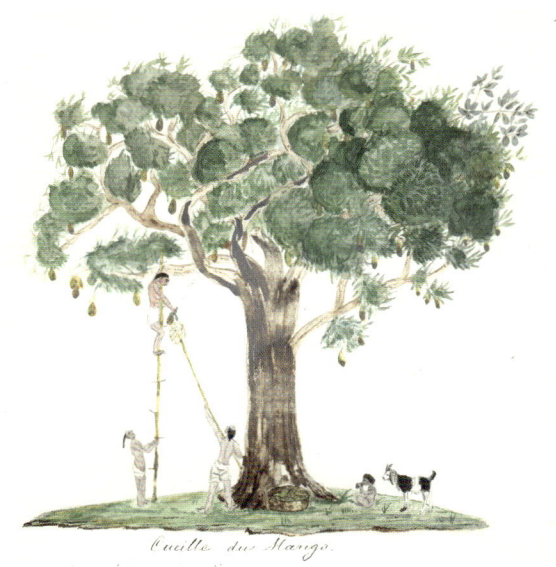

Cueille du Mango.

Fig. 6
Gathering Mangoes.
Drawing by Antoine Marie Gachet ("Asian Diary," p. 23).
Courtesy of the Capuchin Friary, Fribourg.

differ much in substance. His pronouncement on their fanaticism is impressive: "I would not be surprised at all if all Europeans of this region would be massacred in a single moment" (MA V: 995f.).

Of course, one has to question why Gachet was unable to transcend his own verdict, already established from the start. Had he been incapable to overcome his disappointment caused by his removal from his beloved Menominees? Or was it simply the result of the circumstances of his life? He was living in mission houses and episcopal institutions but not really among the Indian population. His regular occupation was that of secretary of the bishop, and as such he was confronted with problems that were pastoral (church services, sermons, visitations, individual pastoral care) or political (schismatic Christianity, British sovereignty with its soldiers and families). One can only marvel at what Gachet was achieving in this respect. For everything else there was not much time left. Yet it must be said that the reality of India was quite different from that of America. In India he was facing complex, multifaceted phenomena, whereas among the Menominees he had encountered a relatively comprehensible and homogenous culture.

He nevertheless time and again made drawings of natural phenomena, plants, animals, people. He also described anthropological and ethnographic differences in complexion, physique, dress, mentality, and behavior of the Indians.[10]

He was especially interested in philological problems. "Hindustani, or rather Urdu, which is a composite of Hindi, Sanskrit, Arabic, and Farsi, is the official language of the country. It is full of vigor and of a wonderful simplicity in its grammatical system. One could say: the French of India, because just as in Europe everyone with a certain amount of education speaks French, every Indian with a certain amount of education speaks Urdu" (MA V: 924). Gachet was fascinated by this language to such an extent that he intended eventually to write a study about it (MA V: 1017). He was wondering about the internal unity of the Indo-European languages and composed a table comparing eight languages: English, Sanskrit, Greek, Latin, "Teutonic," Celtic, Hindustani, and Arabic (MA V: 1017). In another table he compiled data on seven Indian languages in the alphabetic Devanagari script together with the corresponding sound values: Devanagari itself, Bengali, Kaithi, Marathi, Oriya, Burmese, and Bhutani (MA V: 1026f.). I am not in a position to decide to what extent this tabulation is scientifically sound and whether it represents Gachet's own achievement. A similar synopsis is featured in Gachet's "Calligraphie Orientale Talik(!)" (MA V: 1027–1030).[11] In his multi-page presentation Gachet successively equates the Nastaliq texts with Western sound values and explains the meaning of each of the dots, loops, sub- and superimpositions, as well as other traits of the writing. These tables stand isolated in volume V of the *Monumenta Anastasiana*. Once again I am not able to pass a judgement on their scientific value.

This examination of Oriental languages required continued efforts. During his voyage to India Gachet studied Arabic for three weeks in Alexandria (MA V: 894). He also improved his knowledge with the help of a Muslim who taught the children Farsi (MA V: 1056). He consistently took an interest in questions of etymology. Thus, e.g., he wondered about the meaning of the famous syllable "Om," the "secret and mysterious word always spoken by the Hindus with the greatest respect," and discusses the two possibilities: Either the syllable is synonymous with our "Amen," or it represents as "AUM" the trinitarian secret of Shiva: to create, preserve, and destroy. Gachet concludes that "there can be no doubt that the Tibetan and the Hindu 'Om' have the same origin" (MA V: 1032).

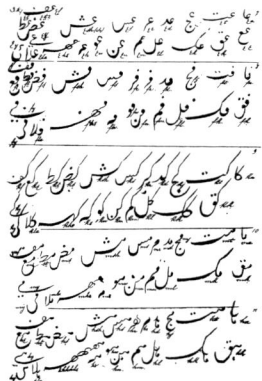

Fig. 7
Taliq calligraphy
(after MA V: 1028).

[11] Taliq is an Arabic-Islamic calligraphy invented during the tenth century in Iran and since the fourteenth century further developed into Nastaliq and passed on to India (https://de.wikipedia.org/wiki/Taliq; https://de.wikipedia.org/wiki/Nastaliq.

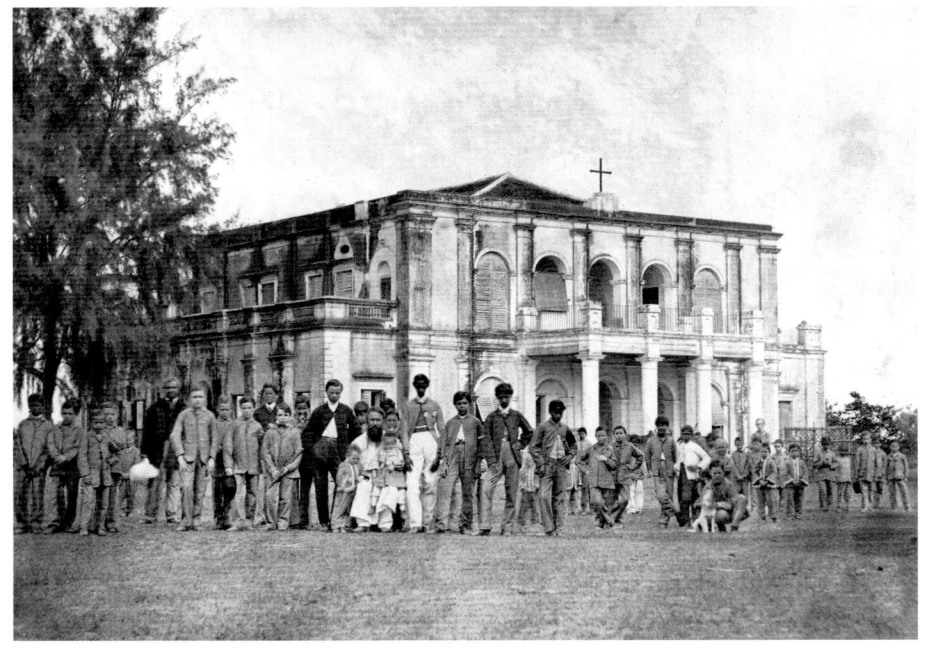

Fig. 8
Antoine Marie Gachet in the midst of orphans adopted into the household of the episcopal residence in Patna.
Unknown photographer, ca. 1865. Courtesy of the Capuchin Friary, Fribourg.

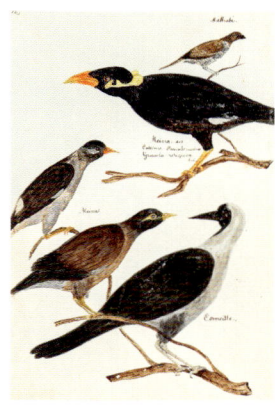

Fig. 9
[Study of birds].
Drawing by Antoine Marie Gachet ("Asian Diary," p. 12). Courtesy of the Capuchin Friary, Fribourg.

A. M. Gachet witnessed the heroic death of his bishop.[12] Soon afterwards and in frail health, he embarked upon his return to Switzerland. But he had made up his mind that he would return to India whenever it was possible. He felt himself so inextricably linked to Anastasius Hartmann that he wanted to die in the country where Hartmann had ended his life (MA V: 1109). He still held to this view when retiring to the Rigi to recuperate his health (MA V: 1167). Here, rather suddenly and without any conclusion, the "Asian Diary" comes to an end.

Twenty-One Years in Switzerland

A. M. Gachet's wish to return to India was not to be fulfilled. Apparently his health would not permit him to do so. Pope Pius IX wanted to send him back to India, as Bishop of Patna-Bombay;[13] the Swiss superior of the order, Bernhard Christen, intended to appoint him as Professor for Languages at the mission college St. Fidelis of Sigmaringen in Rome; and the state of Fribourg had him in mind as Rector of the Gymnasium St. Michael. Gachet declined all of these offers (Grangier 1891). The obituary also points out that Gachet had donated about 50 Menominee objects to the Museum of Antiquities of the canton of Fribourg.[14]

At first Gachet served as vicar and from 1872 to 1875 as guardian in Fribourg, and he subsequently held various functions alternately in Sion (Sitten) and Fribourg. In 1872 he was elected to the provincial council of the Swiss Capuchins and in 1885 appointed "lector" (professor of theology) in Sion. During this period of time (as documented in the records of the friary's archive) he investigated further linguistic relationships (Chinese and Hebrew) and was planning to write a book on general linguistics. He contemplated the idea of expressing his ongoing attachment to India by publishing the autobiography and works of the Carthusian monk Dom Herman and sending the proceeds to India. And he also wanted to add to his "American Diary" a history of the American Capuchin province. On 1 February 1890 Antoine Marie Gachet passed away in full consciousness in the friary of his beloved native city.

[12] Cp. Gachet's reports in French and in German in MA V: 327–449; also his French letter to the procurator of missions on the same subject, combined with his request for permission to return to Switzerland for reasons of health.

[13] According to Fidelis Stöckli, the combined mention of Patna and Bombay is rather doubtful for ecclesiopolitical and geographical reasons. After 1860 the two cities were no longer connected under ecclesiastical law.

[14] For a discussion of this question in the light of surviving documents, see pp. 37–39 in this volume.

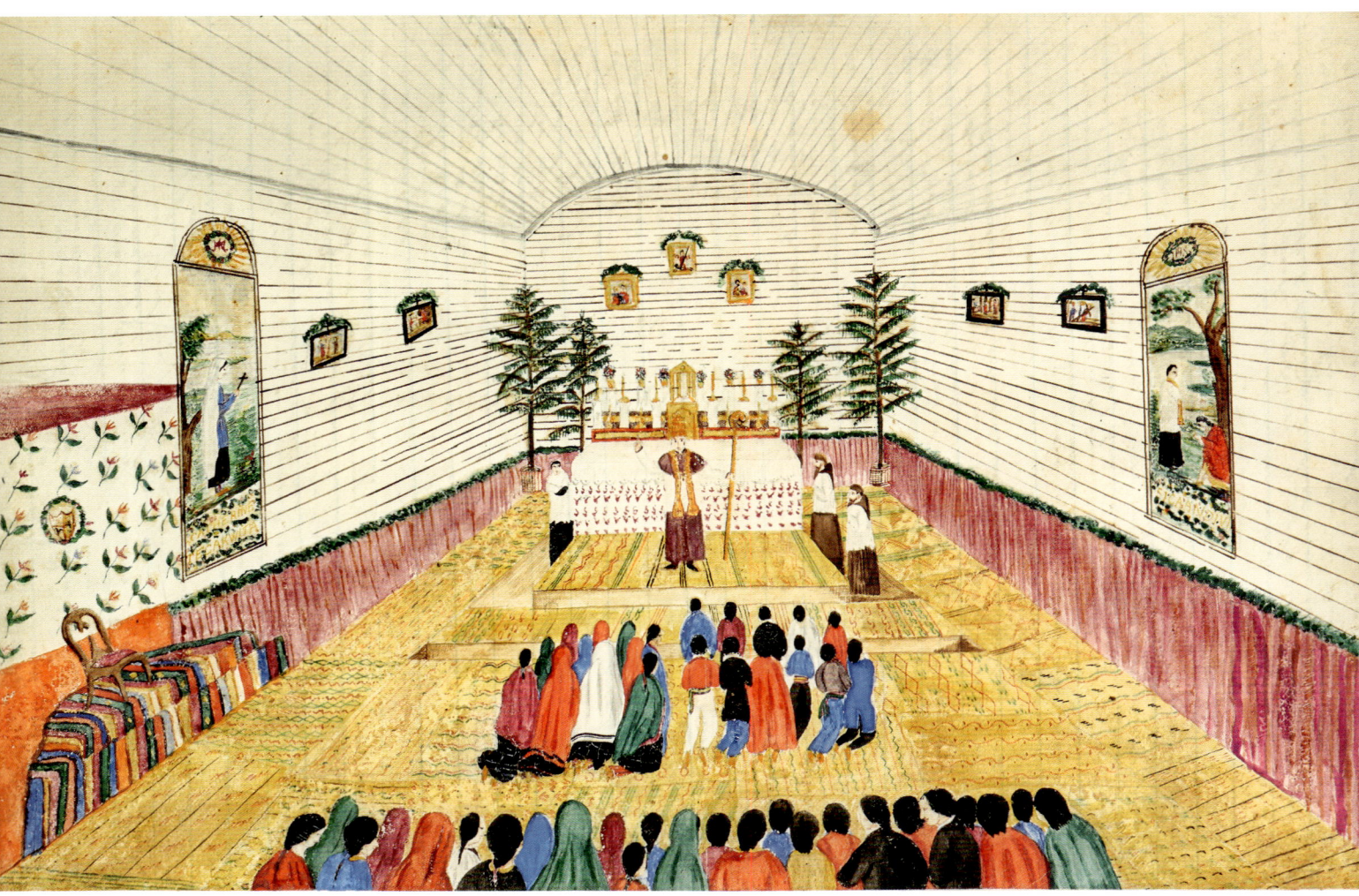

Fig. 10
[Pastoral visit of Bishop Henni to the Catholic Menominee community in the church of Keshena, Wisconsin, 18 October 1860]. Drawing by Antoine Marie Gachet ("American Diary," p. 200). Courtesy of the Capuchin Friary, Fribourg.

The visit of John Martin Henni, the first Catholic bishop of Milwaukee, was an event of major significance for Menominee Catholics. After mass and communion in the morning, mothers brought their children to receive the bishop's blessings. In the afternoon 230 Menominees received the sacrament of confirmation. Gachet's only regret was Bishop Henni's refusal to partake of the beaver tail especially prepared by the Menominees for the dinner in his honor (Gachet 1890: 257–258).

Several layers of the finest rush mats were covering the floor, and in addition to small pictures of the Stations of the Cross along the walls, two large transparent banners depicting the Mohawk Saint Kateri Tekakwitha and the baptism of an Indian, painted by Gachet in March 1860, hung in front of the windows (Gachet 1890: 227, 238). Next to the image of Kateri, a dais surmounted by a canopy had been erected for the bishop.

ANTOINE MARIE GACHET:
Missionary Ethnographer among the Menominees, 1859–1862

[1] I am indebted to Professor François Ruegg for inviting me to reinvestigate Gachet's ethnographic collection and for making this publication possible. I am also deeply grateful to the late Anton Rotzetter, OFM Cap, for alerting me in 2014 to Gachet's drawings preserved in the archive of the Capuchin Friary in Fribourg and for facilitating access for research. The generous permission of the Capuchin Friary in Fribourg to photograph and publish these images is likewise gratefully acknowledged.

Christian Feest, who first brought Gachet's collection to my attention in 1989, commented on numerous earlier drafts of this book, which has profited immensely from his suggestions.

[2] This was most likely Capt. William Powell, who intermittently served in this function in the late 1850s and 1860s (Beck 2002: 209; RCIA 1858: 32).

"I am perfectly happy here and altogether in my element," Antoine Marie Gachet confidently declared in a letter to Bishop Martin Henni two months after his arrival on the Menominee Reservation (Gachet 1859: [1r]).[1] Taking over the vacant mission post had been the fulfilment of a long-cherished desire, for which the Capuchin father had carefully prepared himself. Months before leaving the friary of Mt. Calvary in Wisconsin, where he served as guardian and master of novices, he had started learning the Ojibwa language with the help of the grammar and dictionary published by Friedrich Baraga (1850, 1853), which the latter, then Bishop of Sault Sainte Marie in Michigan, had sent him (Gachet 1858; 1890: 77).

Gachet and his confrère, lay brother Vinzenz Engel, arrived in Keshena on 1 June 1859 after a two-week trip on foot and by steamboat. The progress of their journey had repeatedly been delayed by the seasonal rafting of logs along Wolf River, forcing the two men to seek the hospitality of fellow missionaries or "Yankee" settlers along the way. During a stopover in New London Gachet read Mass for the German and Polish immigrants of this small frontier settlement. He also put idle time to good use by committing to paper his acute observations of the scenery, fauna, and flora—not failing to point out the importance of wild rice as a staple of Menominee subsistence and the origin of their old French designation "Folles Avoines" ('people of the wild oats'). Making the acquaintance of fellow travelers on board the steamboat, like the government interpreter for the Menominees[2] and especially Charles Grignon, a member of one of the most influential local trader families of Franco-Canadian descent, proved opportune, but it was the first sight of Native people that made Gachet's heart beat faster: The Menominee families gliding downstream in their dugout canoes, their faces "painted in striking colors," returned his curiosity by regarding him "with the most lively attention." Upon arrival at their destination Gachet and Brother Vinzenz were greeted both by "pagan"[3] bystanders draped in their traditional blankets, who watched them with "a superb indifference," and by the enthusiastic welcome of Christian Menominees, who asked for benediction and provided them with the first necessities of daily life in their new home (Gachet 1890: 120–133).

These first impressions recorded in Gachet's diary clearly reveal that the geographical and cultural setting of his new activities was far from a pristine wilderness inhabited by indigenous peoples untouched by European civilization. At the time he and Brother Vinzenz set up house in Keshena, the Menominees and their indigenous neighbors already looked back on two centuries of cultural interaction with Europeans, which had left indelible traces both on their land, their ways of life, and their religious beliefs.

At the time of first contact with French fur traders in 1667 the Menominees were living near the mouth of the Menominee River, where according to their origin myth the Great White Bear had ascended from the underworld and turned into the first man. Hunting in the vast expanses of forest west of Lake Michigan, fishing in the numerous streams and lakes, and the gathering of wild plants provided the basis of their subsistence, which was supplemented by corn and vegetables cultivated by the women during the summer months and the harvesting of wild rice in the fall. The Menominees shared many cultural traits with other Algonquian-speaking neighbors, like the Chippewas, Ottawas, or Potawatomis, but also with the Siouan-speaking Winnebagoes, with whom they maintained close relations.

During French and (after 1763) British colonial rule Indian-White relations were governed by military alliances and fur trade interests, which embroiled the Native peoples in the colonial wars fought by the European powers and drew them into dependence on imported trade goods. The decline of game due to the ever increasing demand for furs entailed adaptations in the Native economic cycles in the form of extended winter hunts or even the migration of whole villages. While the first encounters with Christianity in the course of Jesuit missionary efforts in the late seventeenth century only left a fleeting impression, the numerous conjugal relations between White traders and Native women resulted in a Métis elite, who acted as cultural brokers and fostered the responsiveness of Native communities to the influence of Western goods and values. Imbalances of power and inevitable cultural changes notwithstanding, the dealings between indigenous people and colonial representatives during this period were largely defined by diplomacy, exchange, mutual respect, and to a considerable extent by personal relations. This was to change profoundly when the territory fell to the United Stated after ratification of the Treaty of Ghent in 1815.

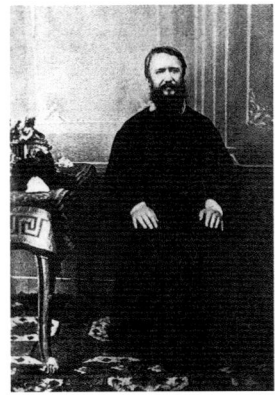

Fig. 11
Antoine Marie Gachet, ca. 1860s.
Undated studio photograph (after MA 1948: opp. 796).

[3] The expressions "pagan" and "heathen" are quoted here with reference to their usage in the historical sources. It has to be noted that "Pagans" or "Pagan party" at the time denoted more than just adherence to a particular belief system, but more generally referred to the social habits and cultural convictions inextricably linked with these beliefs. Especially in administrative jargon the terms were thus used to designate one of the two opposing political camps in Menominee society (cp. p. 27 below).

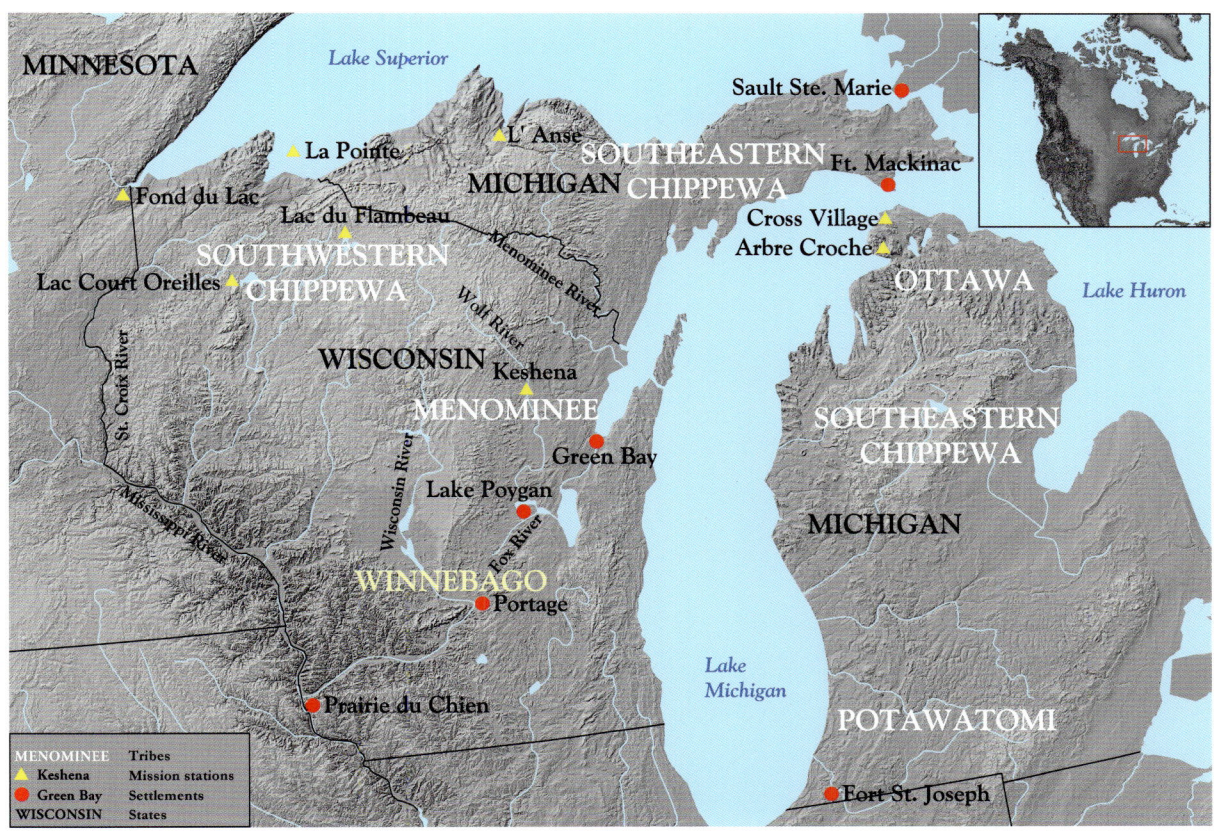

Fig. 12
The western Great Lakes
area in the nineteenth
century.
Copyright: Christian Feest.

Under U.S. administration the Menominees and their indigenous neighbors saw themselves confronted with an unprecedented and aggressive assimilation policy, which aimed at their fast integration into White society. The concerted efforts to "civilize" the aboriginal inhabitants of the country were directly linked

Fig. 13
Menominee Village.
Colored lithograph (after
Castelnau 1842: Pl. 22).

Apart from the characteristic dome-shaped dwellings covered with rush mats, Castelnau's plate shows both kinds of watercraft in use by the Menominees (a birchbark canoe with sail in the background and a dugout canoe in front), a rush mat in the process of weaving, as well as a cradleboard (in which, however, the child is placed upside down).

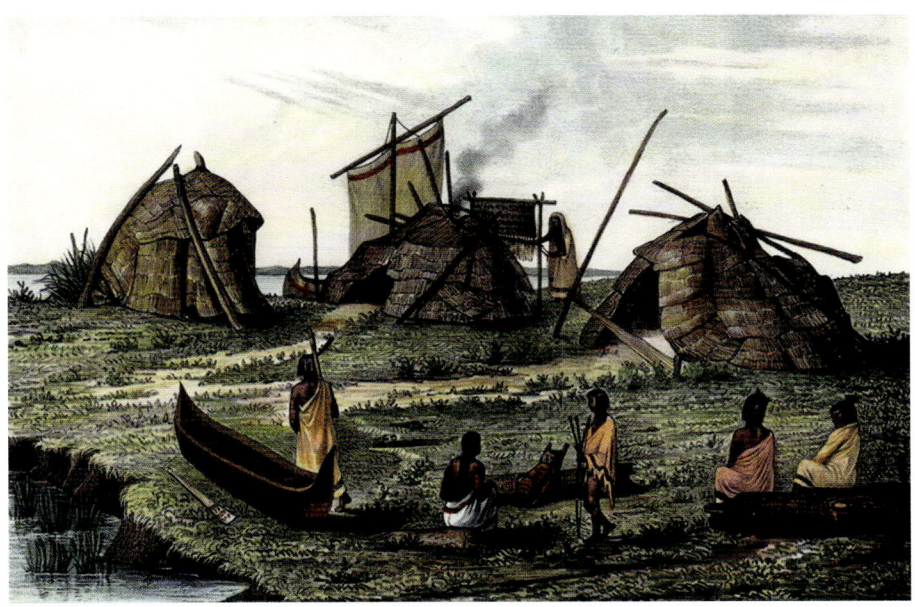

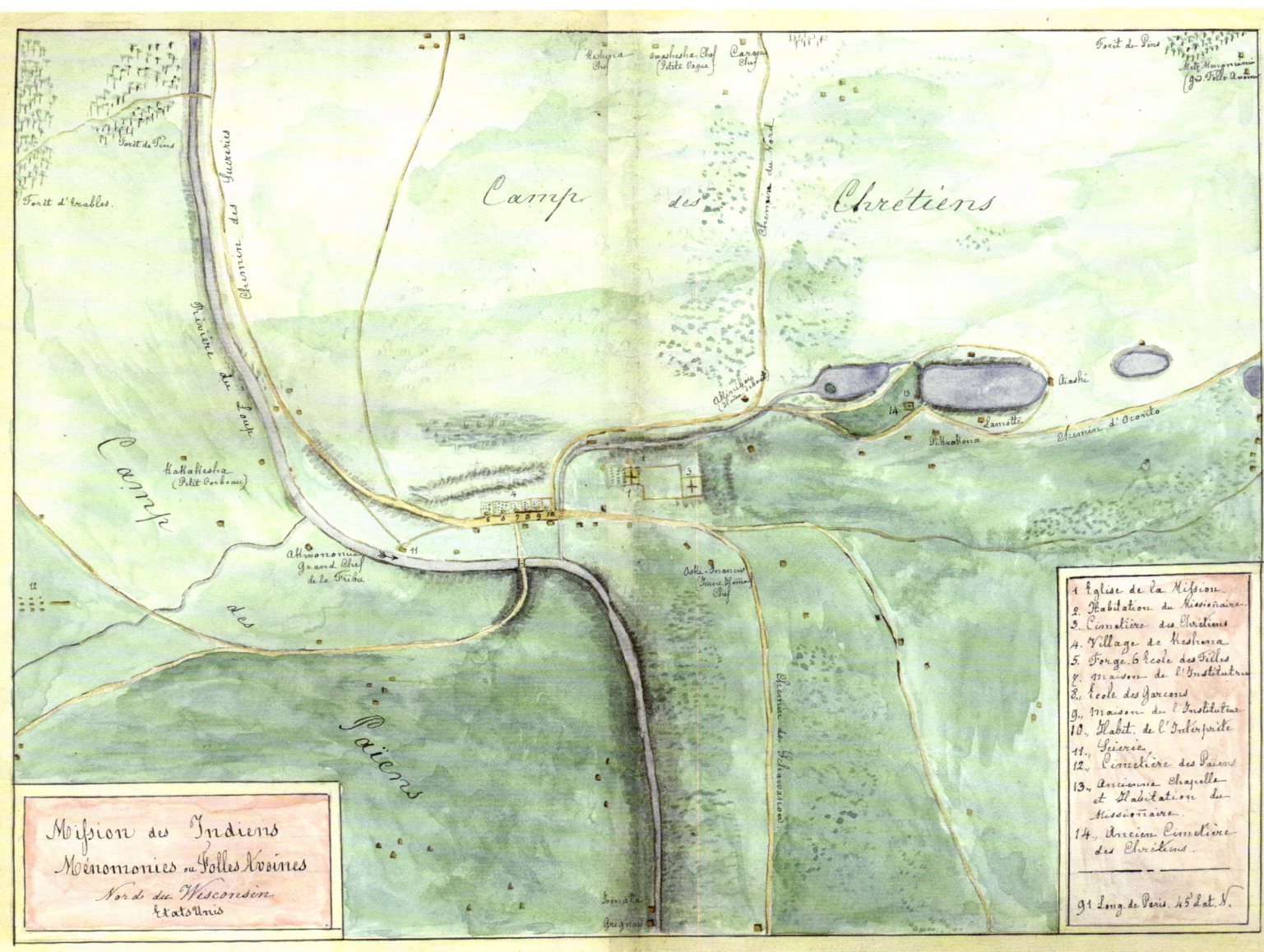

Fig. 14
Mission of the Menominee Indians or Folles Avoines, Northern Wisconsin, United States.
Drawing by Antoine Marie Gachet ("American Diary," p. 97). Courtesy of the Capuchin Friary, Fribourg.

Gachet's map depicts the main village Keshena (4) and adjacent parts of the Menominee Reservation. Centrally located are the mission church (1), the home of the missionary (2), the Christian cemetery (3), and a little further west the blacksmith shop (5), girls' school (6), boys' school (8), and the houses of the female teacher (7), male teacher (9), and interpreter (10). Gachet furthermore indicated the separate settlement areas of the Christian converts (to the north and east of Keshena) and the "Pagans" (west of the Wolf River) and marked the dwellings of some of the more prominent chiefs and leaders.

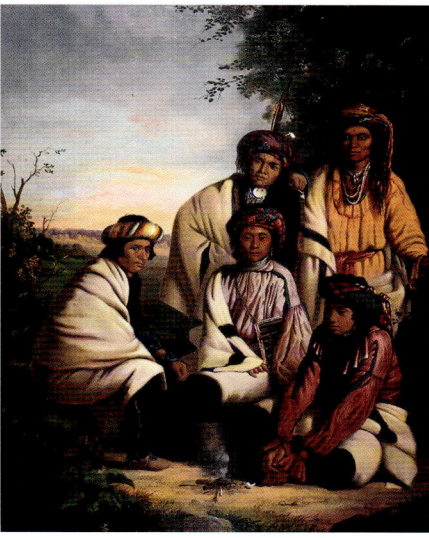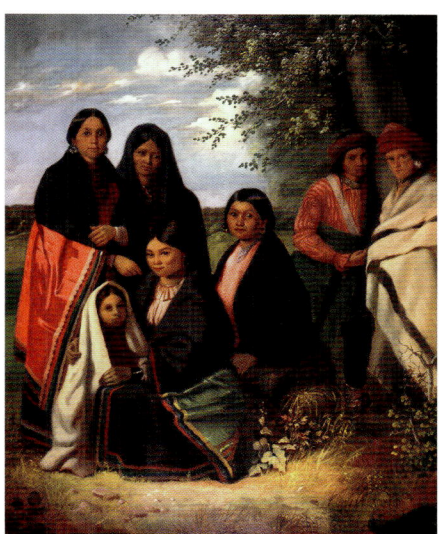

Figs. 15 and 16
Samuel Marsden Brookes, *Group of Menominee Men* (left), *Group of Menominee Women* (right).
Oil on canvas, 1858. Courtesy of the Milwaukee Public Museum, #50403 and #65663.

Brookes's female subjects are not identified, but the artist noted the names of the men on the back of the canvas: Ne-kun-a-quok, Kis-kan-a-keom, and Na-ke-wai-mi seated in front, Na-a-nos-a-ko-sa and Tik-ko standing behind them. Both men and women are dressed in typical "Indian fashion" of the time, combining ready-made trade and gift items such as blankets or ruffled shirts with Native-made garments such as moccasins or leggings, skirts, and shawls manufactured from wool cloth and silk obtained in trade.

4 Between 1836 and 1850 Wisconsin's Euroamerican population grew from 11,683 to 305,390 (A. Smith 1973: 460). In contrast, the 1838 outbreak of small pox alone caused the deaths of about one third of the Menominee population, which dwindled from an estimated 4,000 in 1820 to about 1,450 in 1880 (Kasprycki 2006: 76–85).

5 For surveys of Menominee tribal history, see Keesing 1987, Ourada 1979, Beck 2002; cp. also White 1991, Bieder 1995.

to the exponentially growing influx of European settlers, who relentlessly pushed the frontier westward. Between 1827 and 1848 the Menominees were pressured into a series of treaties, by which they ceded practically all of their tribal land. Successful lobbying in Washington, energetically supported by the Belgian missionary Florimond Bonduel then stationed among the Menominees, eventually spared them the impending relocation west of the Mississippi. In 1852 the main body of the tribe started resettling on a tiny fraction of their ancestral homeland bordering on Wolf River, which in 1854—five years before Gachet's arrival on the scene—was finally granted them as a reservation (Fig. 14).

The gradual loss of land and political autonomy was accompanied by a traumatic loss of lives: While the numbers of White settlers in Wisconsin multiplied, the Menominees suffered a dramatic population decline due to endemic outbreaks of small pox, cholera, and other imported diseases throughout the nineteenth century.[4] The pervading existential crisis experienced in the wake of these constant threats to their social, cultural, and biological survival led many Menominees to explore the potential power of the teachings offered by Christian missionaries.[5]

Missionary endeavors in the Great Lakes region, which had lain dormant for more than a hundred years after the first Jesuit forays in the seventeenth century, were reawakened with the advent of United States supremacy in the area. Due to the lack of funds and personnel both for the pastoral care of the burgeoning communities of European immigrants and for missionary work among the Native peoples, Protestant as well a Catholic churches depended heavily on the support of European missionary societies during the first decades of the nineteenth century. One of the organizations that became influential for the Catholic mission among the Menominees (and in the Great Lakes region in general) was the

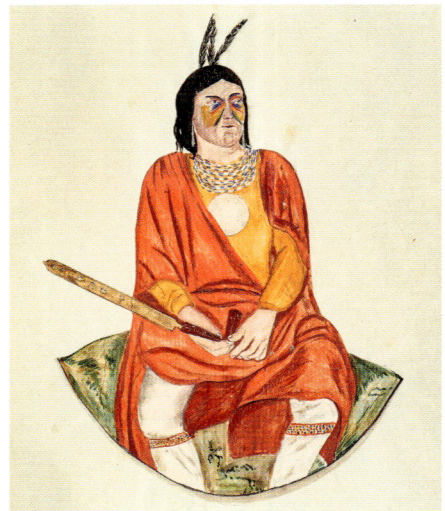 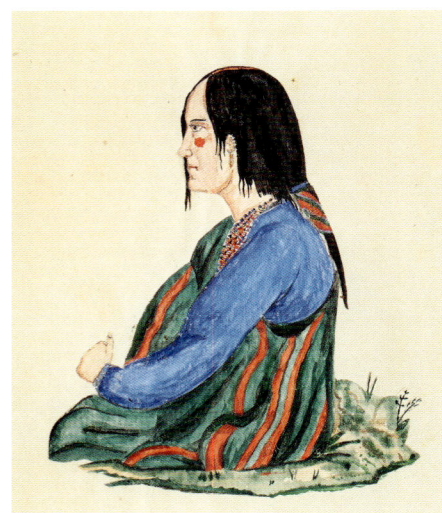

Figs. 17 and 18
Indian War Chief (left) and
Pagan Indian Woman (right).
Drawings by Antoine Marie
Gachet ("American Diary,"
pp. 207 and 209). Cour-
tesy of the Capuchin Friary,
Fribourg.

Facial painting was one of
the most conspicuous out-
ward signs by which "tradi-
tionalists" distinguished
themselves from Christian
converts: "The women
have given up the old cus-
tom of painting red their
faces and hair and nowa-
days are content with a red
streak across the cheeks
and at the line of separa-
tion of their hair. The men
continue to paint their
faces in various colors,
which gives them a
hideous appearance"
(Gachet 1890: 268).

Austrian Leopoldine Foundation (Kummer 1966), which financed the pioneer-
ing work of Friedrich Baraga, who inspired a great number of missionary followers, and which also provided substantial monetary and material support as well
as publicity for the labors of Gachet's predecessors among the Menominees. As
elsewhere, Protestants and Catholics were competing for Menominee converts,
but despite the pronounced bias of U.S. government officials toward the anglo-
phone missionaries of the Episcopal Church active during the first years of
renewed missionary efforts, Christianization of the Menominees firmly remained
in the hands of Catholic priests from continental Europe throughout the major
part of the nineteenth century.

Despite its overt success, however, the Catholic Menominee mission suffered from a considerable turnover of staff, which was due to insufficient funds,
changing policies of the responsible diocese(s) or religious orders, opposition of
government agents, and a number of other reasons. After the Italian Dominican
priest Samuele Mazzuchelli had initiated the building of a church and a school
house for the Menominees in Green Bay in the early 1830s, the Redemptorist
fathers Simon Sänderl from Bavaria and Franz Hätscher from Austria headed the
Menominee mission there with interruptions up to 1837. In 1835 the Dominican father Theodoor J. van den Broek from the Netherlands founded a new mission post some twenty-five miles away from Green Bay in Little Chute on the
Fox River, which grew into a sizeable village with church, school houses, barns,
stables, and cultivated farmland. The fate of his successful enterprise was, however, sealed by the stipulations of the land cession agreed to by the Menominees
in 1836, which eventually forced the blooming Catholic community to move
further west and resettle on Lake Poygan. There the aging Dutch missionary was
replaced by the Belgian priest Florimond Bonduel, who served the Menominee
Catholics between 1846 and 1854 and after further land cessions migrated with

[6] After Gachet's unexpected recall in 1862, the short-lived missionary terms among the Menominees were continued with intermissions by the Capuchin fathers Cajetan Krauthahn and Fidelis Steinauer and the Belgian priest Amandus Masschelein, before the Franciscan Province of the Sacred Heart took charge of the mission in 1880 and—backed with greater financial and personal resources—ushered in a period of stability extending into the twentieth century.

For a study of the cultural interaction between Menominees and Catholic missionaries and the role of material culture in the processes of Christianization, see Kasprycki 2006.

[7] The term is used following Comaroff and Comaroff 1991.

his congregation from Lake Poygan to what was to become the Menominee Reservation. Bonduel's successor and Gachet's immediate predecessor was the Franciscan priest Otto Skolla from Slovenia, who after a brief spell at a mission outpost among Menominees on the Oconto River superseded Bonduel in Keshena, where he remained in charge of the mission until 1857.[6]

Regardless of denomination, religious order, or individual cultural empathy, missionaries shared a common concept of "Christian civilization," which implicitly or explicitly informed their agenda. Their historically grounded religious convictions were intrinsically linked to other cultural domains, and while they ostensibly aimed at transforming indigenous beliefs by spreading the "universal truth" of God's word, they also conveyed their own culture-specific values, norms, and habits and not only converted to Christianity, but also to agriculture as a means of subsistence, European styles of dress, Western house forms, and social rules acceptable to the dominant society. It was this gradual "colonization of consciousness"[7] that made the Catholic missionaries accomplices of U.S. assimilation policies, even though the European priests—themselves considered "aliens" by U.S. administrators—often and outspokenly critized the U.S. government's treatment of Native peoples. The Menominee converts, who followed their own culturally motivated interests in approaching Christianity, accepted the offer part and parcel. When Gachet arrived on the reservation, Menominee society was already divided into a Christian and a "Pagan" party, who not only differed in their religious affiliations but also in their adherence to the respective modes of dress, economic activities, and lifestyles.

Gachet set out with fervor to consolidate the work of his predecessors, renewing the vows of baptism, consecrating marriages, hearing confessions, and making his pastoral rounds in order to get to know and gain the trust of his new

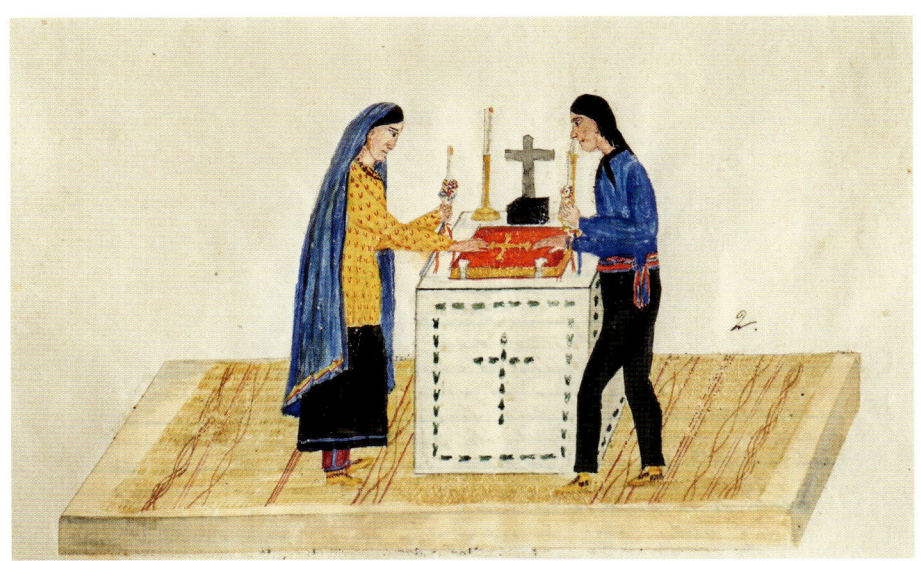

Fig. 19
Renewing of the Vows of Baptism at the Day of First Communion.
Drawing by Antoine Marie Gachet ("American Diary," p. 173). Courtesy of the Capuchin Friary, Fribourg.

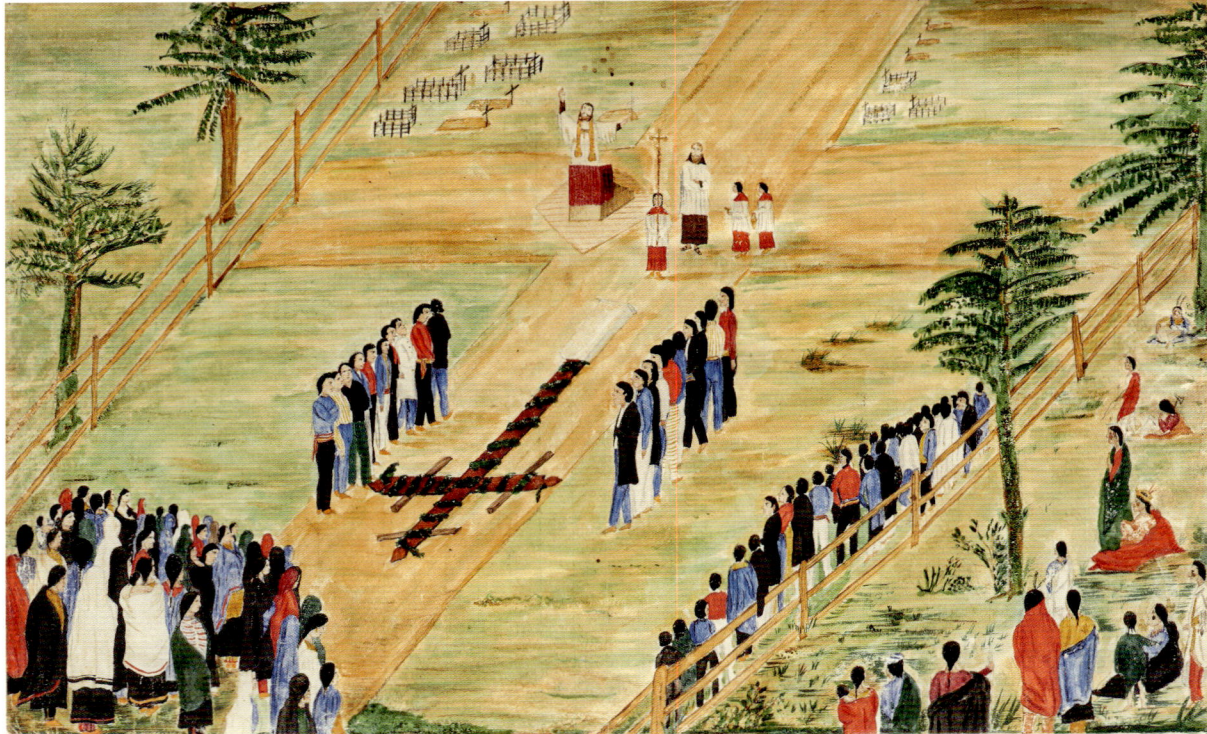

Fig. 20
Erection of the Cross in the Cemetary.
Drawing by Antoine Marie Gachet ("American Diary," p. 188). Courtesy of the Capuchin Friary, Fribourg.

Apart from the regular Catholic feast days, numerous other events like baptisms, burials, supplicatory processions, or the consecration of buildings or objects filled the ritual calendar of the Menominee congregation. Gachet was quick to point out that these festivities regularly attracted numerous "pagan" spectators—represented here on the right outside the fence—whose curiosity he attributed to the irresistible appeal of these "beautiful ceremonies" (Gachet 1890: 130, 173, 245).

While the dress of the Christian women remained closer to traditional models, the male converts are shown in shirts, trousers, and the occasional black coat. The onlookers from the "traditionalist" camp all wear facial paint and are distinguished by their preference for trade blankets, feather-ornamented headdresses, and accessories like bows and arrows or pipe tomahawks.

congregation. Motivated by the realization that many Menominees, especially of the younger generation, were no longer fluent in Ojibwa, which had in earlier decades functioned as a *lingua franca* in the area, he started to learn Menominee and by Easter 1861 was able for the first time to preach in this language without the help of an interpreter (Gachet 1861: 1r; 1890: 280). Religious instruction nonetheless remained difficult, not the least due to the intricacies of translating Christian concepts into the native language. Gachet's explanation of the Menominee terms for the Catholic sacraments, for example, clearly reveals the conceptual links to traditional notions that were underlying the respective translations (Gachet 1890: 303).[8] The extent of the converts' intellectual comprehension of Catholic dogma could thus hardly be verified, and in many respects it was their participation in Catholic rituals that was taken as evidence of their faith. Gachet relied on the redemptive power of the sacraments where words might prove

[8] The Menominee word for communion, e.g., rendered by Gachet (1890: 303) as "nikeshshawenik-takoshim" (cp. *sawɛ·neh-takosew*, 'he is pitied, blessed'; *sawɛ·neme-ko·wesew*, 'he is pitied, blessed, given good fortune by the higher powers'; Bloomfield 1975: 230, 231) clearly opens a conceptual link to traditional practices of establishing rapport with supernatural beings by evoking their pity (cp. Skinner 1913: 42–51).

[9] Protestant polemics for the same reason often decried indigenous Catholicism as nothing more than "baptized heathenism" (cp. Berkhofer 1976: 57–60).

[10] On this distinction, see Merrill 1993: 153–154.

[11] Prophylactic health care, the healing of the sick, and the passing on of medicinal knowledge was the domain of the Medicine Society (metɛ·wen) and its practitioners. Shaking tent ritualists (ce·qsahkowak) summoned their spirit helpers to specially built structures in order to diagnose illness, foretell the future, or give information about distant people or events. The activities of Wabeno ritualists (wa·panowak), probably the least understood category of religious specialists, were closely related to warfare; while they also possessed healing powers, their hunting and love charms and especially their spectacular displays of personal power (like immunity to heat) were often seen as "black magic" by outsiders.

For ethnographic studies of Menominee religion, see Hoffman 1896, Skinner 1913, 1915a, b, 1920, 1921; Densmore 1932; cp also Krusche 1981.

insufficient, and like his precursors he placed great confidence in the communicative potential of the Catholic ceremonies. He considered the appeal of their material splendor a clear advantage over the "cold expressions" of Protestant religious observances, which to him seemed "far from satisfying the religious aspirations" of the Native people (Gachet 1890: 256; cp. also 264–265; Fig. 20).[9] The Menominees on their part attached greater importance to the correctness of ritual action ("orthopraxy") than to conformity with abstract teachings ("orthodoxy").[10] While it may be suspected that their understandings of Catholic rituals were not always in accordance with official doctrine, the shared *practice* of religion established a "middle ground" that allowed Native participants to identify with the new religion and tap its spiritual power and at the same time provided an opportunity for the missionary to impart further knowledge.

Gachet's ethnographic investigations of Menominee religion led him to agree with Mazzuchelli's declaration (1915: 57–58) that they were "well disposed by nature to become followers of Jesus Christ." He classified their belief system as a "vestibule of Christianity," based on their veneration of a Supreme Being, their recognition of the existence of subordinate "good and evil spirits," and their idea of an afterlife (Gachet 1890: esp. 173–174). The Menominees' notion of Mɛ·c-awɛ·tok, the 'Great Spirit', had already been interpreted by Gachet's predecessors as a general idea of God (e.g., Mazzuchelli 1915: 56)—a reading that had over time contributed to the personalization of this originally rather vague concept. In a similar vein, missionary equations of the upperworld and underworld of the Menominee cosmos with the Christian concepts of heaven and hell had long served as conceptual bridges in the instruction of converts, even though this imputed moral distinction between "good" and "evil" was alien to Native beliefs, which rather strove for an equilibrium of forces in the universe. The misunderstanding of the indigenous concept of an essentially neutral spiritual power, which could be used for the benefit as well as to the detriment of people, also underlies Gachet's distinction between "good medicine men" or healers, i.e. the functionaries of the Medicine Society, and "bad medicine men" like "prophets" and "magicians," i.e. shaking tent and Wabeno ritualists (Gachet 1890: 184–188).[11]

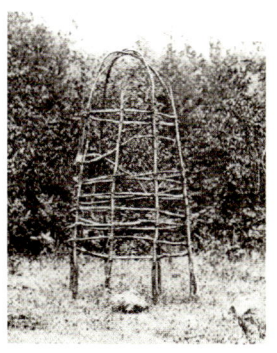 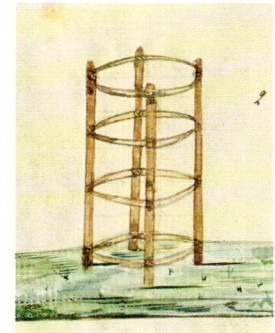

Figs. 21 and 22
Structure of a Menominee Shaking Tent (left).
Photograph (after Skinner 1915a: 193, fig. 2).
Sacred Wigwam (right).
Drawing by Antoine Marie Gachet ("American Diary," p. 147).
Courtesy of the Capuchin Friary, Fribourg.

"On an excursion I made on 9 April [1860] down along the Wolf River I found, half hidden in the bushes, one of those sacred wigwams in which our jugglers invoke the spirits. It was about two meters high by one in diameter" (Gachet 1890: 233).

Gachet further stressed the Menominees' "natural penchant" for religious contemplation and felt convinced that the ease with which they established contact with the supernatural in dreams and visions only needed missionary guidance to lead them to the recognition of the true God. He ascribed the practices of fasting and sacrificing so deeply entrenched in Native culture to a "religious instinct" that predestined them to appreciate Christian religious observances. While the specific forms of Native sacrificial offerings were regarded as "superstitious," they were also seen as a basis for the Menominees' understanding of Jesus Christ's sacrifice and the concept of transsubstantiation (Gachet 1890: 182–184, 227, 265, 279; cp. Mazzuchelli 1915: 110).

Such analogies drawn between indigenous and Christian concepts and practices not only served missionary strategies but also suited Menominee attempts to make sense of the new religion within their own epistemological horizon. They also, however, tended to obscure one of the most significant differences between the two belief systems. For the Catholic missionaries life in this world was only the preliminary stage of a transcendental new order of being that would eventually let true believers partake in the glory of God. Menominee religious practices distinctly focused on the here and now and aimed at maintaining balance and harmony in the universe, on which the sources of their existence depended.

The incentive to engage in a cultural dialogue with Christian missionaries was undeniably brought about by the impact of the colonial encounter, and the long-term consequences of this rapprochement could hardly be foreseen by those involved at the time. Nonetheless the Menominees were far from passive

[12] The disruption of traditional religious systems in the wake of such crises was a frequent occurrence in Native America, often followed by revitalization movements. Experimentation with Christianity was often part of this attempt at "symbolic reconstitution" and proved fertile ground for cultural change (cp. Morrison 1990).

As the Menominee case shows, however, conversion to Christianity was not an irreversible step: Renunciation due to disillusionment with its "efficacy" was not uncommon, and Native movements like the Dream Dance (after 1880) or the Peyote Religion (after 1914) won over many Menominee Catholics—eventually leading to further social and religious pluralization (Hoffman 1896: 157–161; Skinner 1915a: 214–215; Spindler and Spindler 1984).

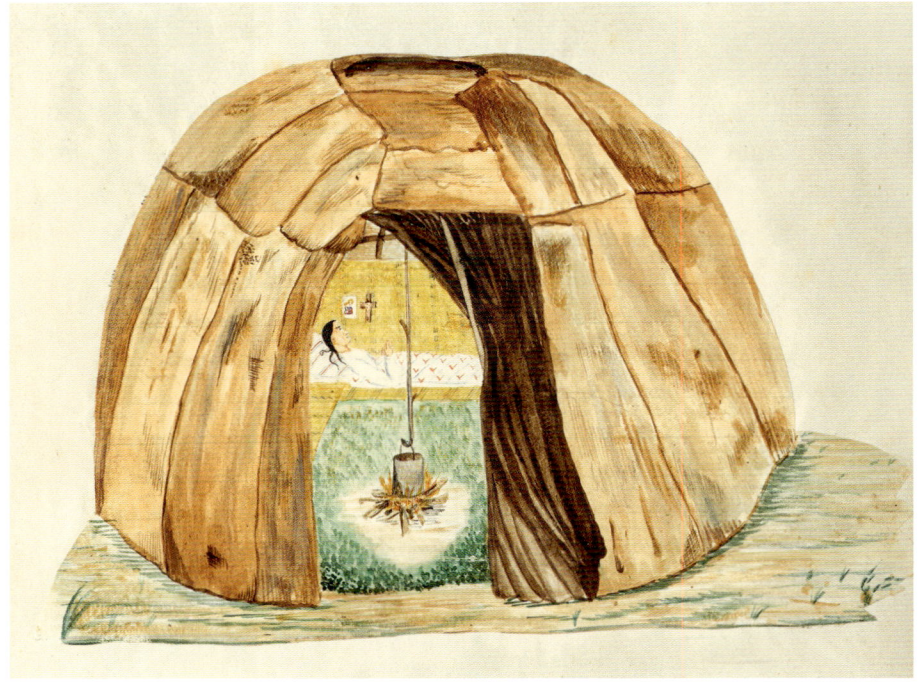

Fig. 23
Marie Metz-mitèmo [on her sickbed].
Drawing by Antoine Marie Gachet ("American Diary," p. 192). Courtesy of the Capuchin Friary, Fribourg.

Gachet baptized Metzmitèmo (cp. *meꞏcetɛmoh*, 'Big Woman'; Bloomfield 1975: 119) shortly before her death in September 1860. Christian women had taken care of the girl during her sickness and had pinned images of saints and a crucifix on the wall next to her bed (Gachet 1890: 249–250).

recipients in this process but rather highly selective customers in search of solutions for specific problems arising from their situation. For some it was strategic access to schooling provided by the missionaries in order to better deal with the increasingly dominant society; for others the missionary temperance societies offered spiritually grounded social reform regarding the widespread abuse of alcohol and its harmful consequences for Native communities. One of the most prominent motivations was rooted in the experience of recurrent disease and the concomitant loss of trust in the ability of traditional religious leaders to cope with this crisis. The Native conception of sickness as a state of disharmony between the individual and his or her social, natural, or supernatural environment persuaded many Menominees to take into consideration what missionaries had to tell them about the "true" world order so as to reestablish balance in the universe.[12]

The Menominees' expectation that the Catholic priests would exercise their power in the realm of health care and healing was only natural in view of the fact that this was one of the most important responsibilities of their own religious experts. Moreover, the missionary strategy of visiting the sick and dying in the hope of "saving souls" before it was too late seemed to confirm this assumption. More than once Gachet found himself in direct competition with traditional healers in such situations, and while baptisms on the sickbed were frequent, they also put the missionary under a certain pressure to "achieve": Many patients and their families anticipated concrete therapeutic effects, and in the end it was recovery that was the final test of the priest's (and his God's) power (Gachet 1861: [2r]; 1890: 248).

The comparatively high death rate after christening, not the least due to the Catholic practice of administering emergency baptism to the mortally ill, had often aroused the suspicion of Native people

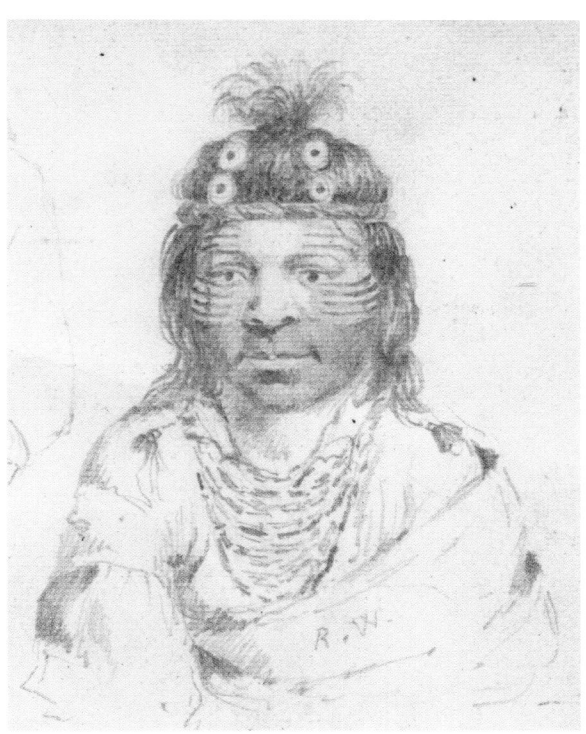

Fig. 24
Paul Kane, *Ac-o-namy*.
Pencil on paper (in *Landscape and Portrait Log*), 1845–1848.
Courtesy of Stark Museum of Art, Orange, Texas, 11.85.4.037.

Aconamy, the eldest son of chief Oshkosh (1795–1858), was in his early twenties when sketched by Paul Kane, who portrays him with roach, facial paint, and wrapped in a trade blanket. The wampum necklaces and profusion of ear ornaments were also noted by Gachet, who met him more than a decade later, when Aconamy had become head chief following his father's death (Gachet 1890: 217). According to the testimony of White contemporaries, Aconamy developed a taste for European fashion in his later life, which is confirmed by photographs showing him in black coat and top hat (Kasprycki 1990a: 90).

(cp. Morrison 1990), and the Menominees still regarded the sacrament with ambivalent feelings in the mid-nineteenth century. When in the spring of 1861 Little Raven, the six-year-old son of head chief Aconamy (Fig. 24), died after having been baptized by Gachet on his sickbed, the Capuchin was seriously concerned that this incident would reinforce "the belief held by the pagans that baptism causes the death of children." Moreover, the little boy's fate also jeopardized the conversion of

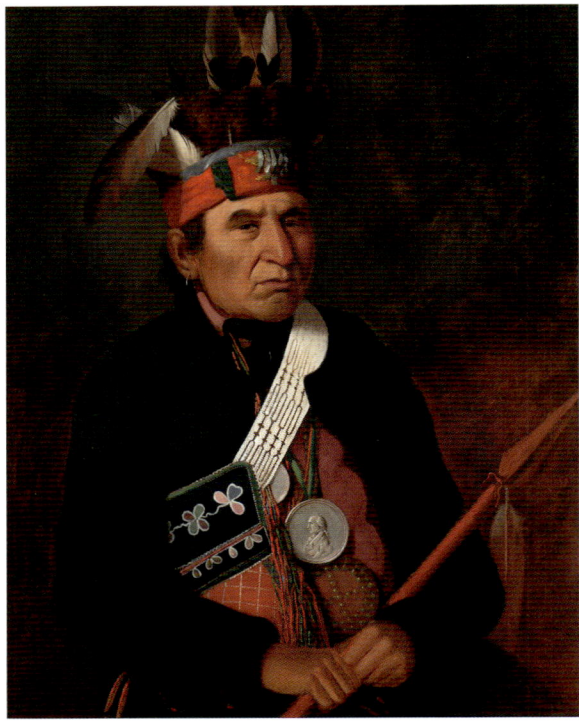 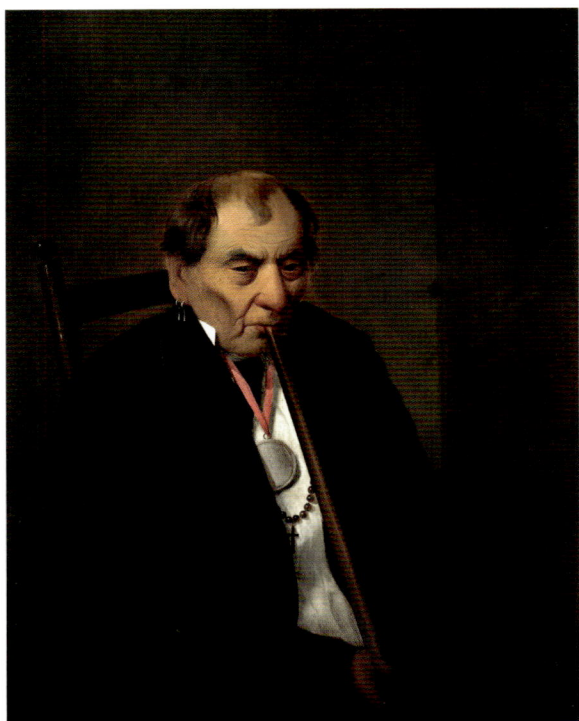

Figs. 25 and 26
Samuel Marsden Brookes, *Souligny* (left) and *Iometah* (right).
Oil on canvas, 1858. Courtesy of the Wisconsin Historical Society, WHS-1868 and WHS-2728.

Brookes was commissioned by the Historical Society of Wisconsin to take the portraits of these two venerated chiefs, and both men had apparently dressed up for the occasion. Souligny, a staunch representative of traditional values, is shown in full regalia with feather-decorated fur turban, bandolier bag, James Madison peace medal, and spear. Gachet had been cautioned that trying to persuade Souligny "to take the prayer" would be like "preaching to a tree," but he took his chances one day in November 1859 when the old war chief lay ill. Souligny graciously but firmly rejected his advances, arguing that even though they would all adore the same Great Spirit, there were different roads laid out for Whites and for Indians to do so (Gachet 1890: 151, 160–161).

Iometah, by then in his eighties, had already converted to Christianity three decades earlier, as is indicated by the rosary worn around his neck. Gachet devoted several pages of his diary to a biography of this much respected leader and relates that during one of his pastoral visits Iometah offered him the pipe tomahawk he had just lit. "I drew a few puffs; never had I smoked better tobacco" (Gachet 1890: 148–150).

Aconamy, who had only a few weeks earlier announced his interest in Christianity. Gachet tried to find consolation in the hope that Little Raven "would bring about in heaven the conversion of his parents," and his prayers were to be heard: Aconamy remained true to his word, and on 2 June 1861 he and three of his followers, together with their wives and children, officially "embraced the faith." Their baptisms in a resplendent ceremony in the church of Keshena constituted the culmination of Gachet's missionary aspirations (cp. Gachet 1861: [1r–1v]; 1862b; 1890: 280, 282, 283–284).

From the very beginning of his sojourn on the Menominee Reservation Gachet proved to be a keen observer of Native customs and material culture,

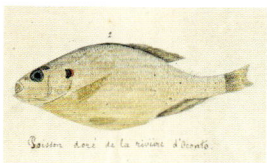

Figs. 27 and 28
Northern Sunfish [Lepomis peltastes] *from the Oconto River* (above) and *Sturgeon Fishing* (right).
Drawings by Antoine Marie Gachet ("American Diary," pp. 423 and 147). Courtesy of the Capuchin Friary, Fribourg.

"The other day […] I had the opportunity to see with what dexterity the Indian knows how to dart the fish. […] To see it, stab it with his spear, and throw it into the bottom of the canoe had been the matter of a second" (Gachet 1890: 234).

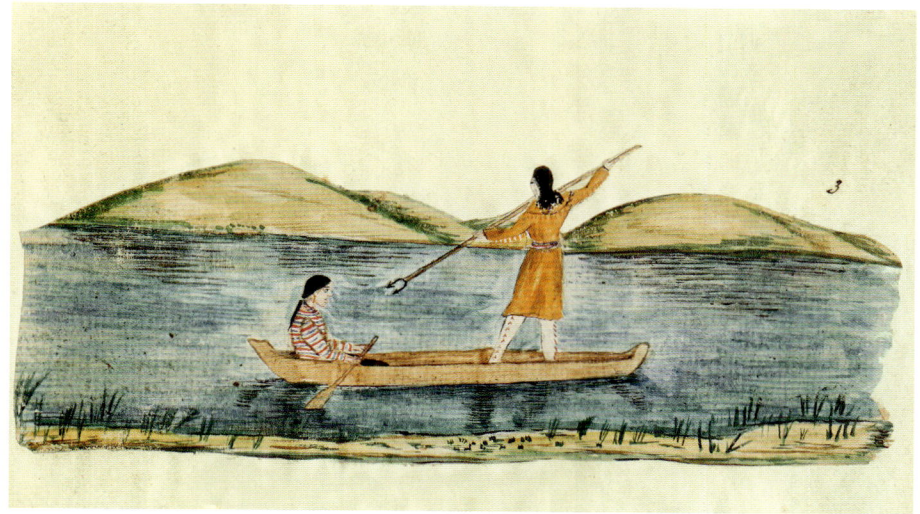

documenting modes of dress, economic activities, traditional house forms, as well as the manufacture of all kinds of products used in daily life in considerable detail. Even though he could not ultimately escape some of the prejudices of his time and station—recognizable by a tinge of ridicule here and there when talking of "backward" habits or by the occasional harsh judgement on customs incompatible with Christian beliefs—Gachet set about his ethnographic studies with serious scholarly intent. He was obviously fascinated with many aspects of Menominee culture and praised their physical skills (Fig. 28), artistic accomplishments, craftsmanship, and technological ingenuity. From his perspective, these qualities were also major assets in the larger scheme of promoting the Menominees' "civilizational progress."

Indigenous forms of subsistence had long been the target of both government and missionary policies of assimilation. "Our object is everywhere the same: To Civilize the Aborigines through the preaching of the Gospel, and by teaching them the Art of Agriculture and Domestic Economy" (Bonduel 1851: 219). Visible advances toward this end had been made under the guidance of Fathers Van den Broek and Bonduel in the Catholic Menominee communities in Little Chute and on Lake Poygan, where the Christian families not only cultivated their own fields but also started to build European-style log houses (cp., e.g., RCIA 1845: 493, 566; 1846: 44–45; 1848: 566, 568–569). These agricultural ventures suffered a severe setback after the forced move to the reservation, where bad soil conditions and adverse weather during the first years occasioned a series of crop failures and frustrated the Native farmers.

Gachet would not have disputed Bonduel's statement and attempted to propagate farming as a God-ordained livelihood and a necessary requirement for an independent economy. At the same time he very clearly realized the Menominee men's deep-rooted aversion against this form of subsistence, which

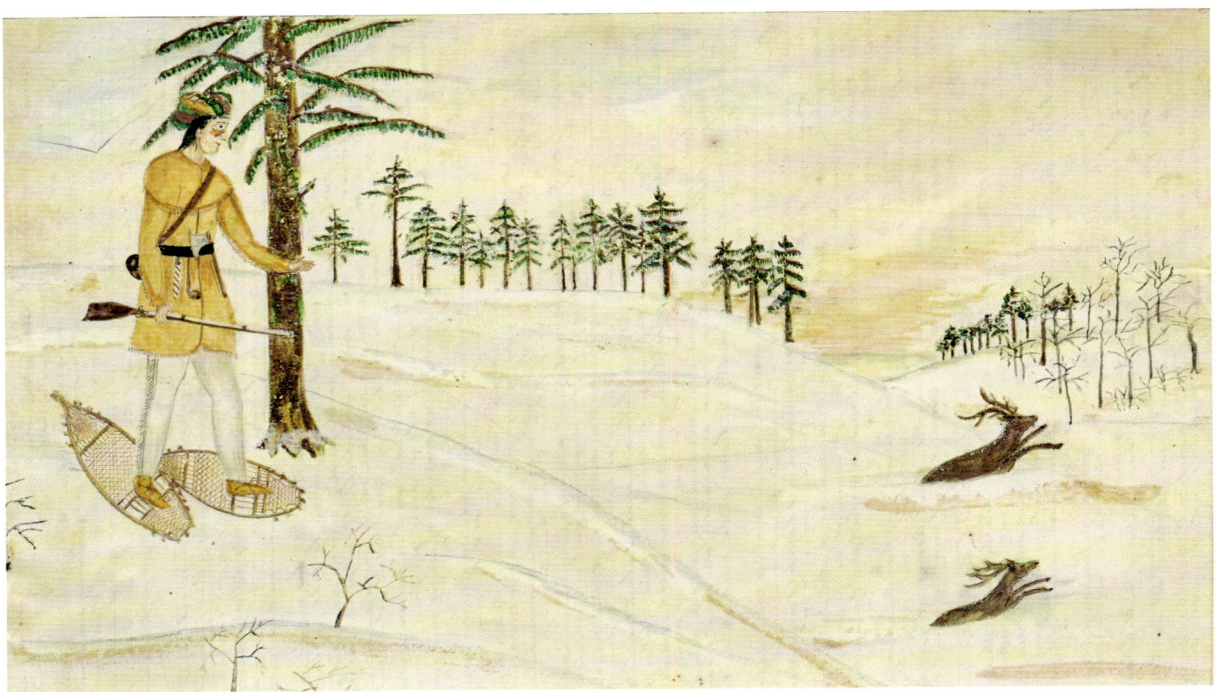

even the Christians could hardly conceal (Gachet 1890: 261). Traditionally, the cultivation of corn and vegetables was women's work and they also processed the game and fish provided by the men, who sought to gain prestige through their prowess as hunters and fishermen (Figs. 29 and 30).[13] Gachet scolded the men for shying away from "rough work," but he could not help admiring the courage, agility, perseverance, and "aristocratic bearing" in their pursuit of traditional economic activities. His romanticized view of hunting as merely a "pastime," widely shared by European observers (cp., e.g., Kohl 1859, 1: 285), tended to underestimate the male contribution to subsistence, while commiserating the women to whose share the major part of work seemingly fell (Gachet 1890: 152, 233, 266, 273). The division of labor by gender found in Menominee society jarred with the accepted roles of men and women in "Christian civilization," and missionaries thus not only preached work ethos but also the ways in which this work was to be properly divided.

The only branch of Native economy unconditionally accepted by the missionaries was the production of maple sugar, even though the prolonged absence of parishioners during the sugar season represented an unwelcome interruption of the daily routines of the congregation. Calendars marking Sundays and feast days were given out to the Menominee Catholics in order to remind them of their religious duties in the seclusion of the sugar camps (cp. Fig. 56 below). Missionary appreciation of sugar making was only partly due to their recognition of the amount of labor put into this tightly organized enterprise, but was primarily influenced by its enormous productivity (Gachet 224–225). The

Fig. 29
Hunting on snowshoes.
Drawing by Antoine Marie Gachet ("American Diary," p. 360). Courtesy of the Capuchin Friary, Fribourg.

Gachet (1890: 262–264) considered the invention of snowshoes a feat of Native ingenuity. He described their construction and also mentioned that the Menominees, "masters of improvisation," knew how to manufacture provisional snowshoes in case of an emergency.

[13] Farming never took hold on the reservation, and Menominee men eventually found in the lumber industry an economic sphere that resembled traditional male work in its seasonality, the cooperation of work groups, and the prestige gained by strength, skill, and courage (Keesing 1897: 184–187, 231).

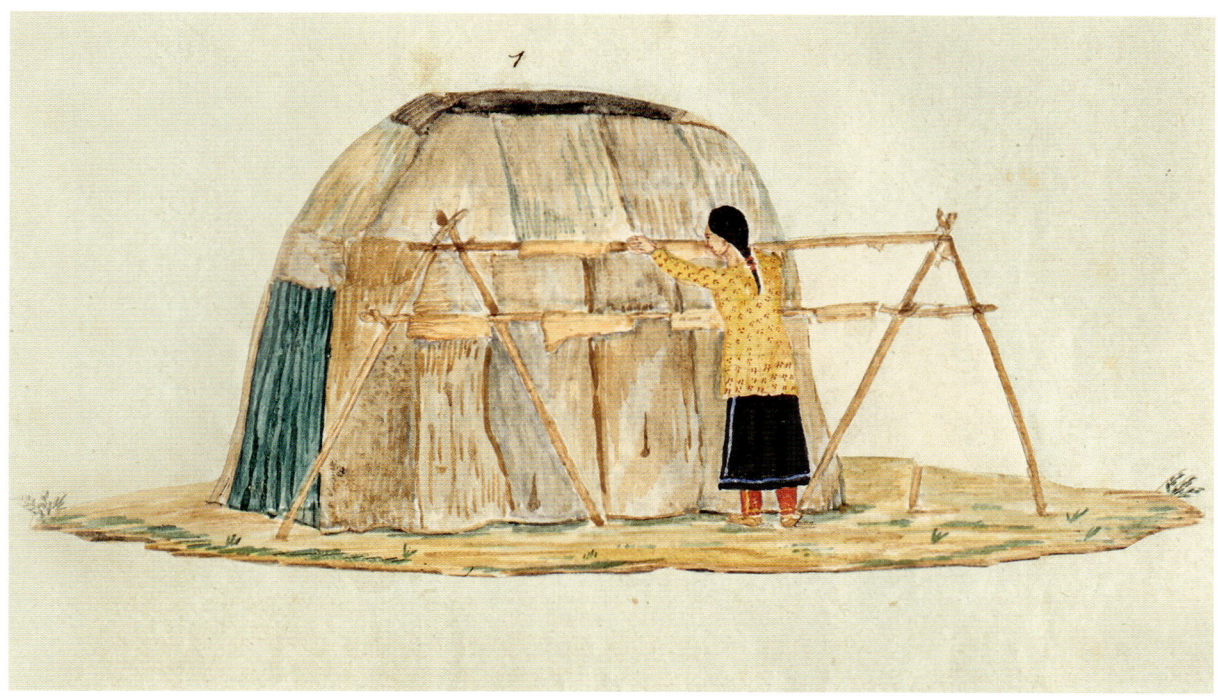

Fig. 30
Bark Wigwam. Indian Woman Drying [Meat or Fish] on a Rack.
Drawing by Antoine Marie Gachet ("American Diary," p. 103). Courtesy of the Capuchin Friary, Fribourg.

Meat and fish were cut into stripes, dried in the sun on wooden frames, and stored as provisions (Gachet 1890: 233–234).

lucrative sale of maple sugar (or its exchange with trade goods) had led to a significant increase of production in the course of the nineteenth century. In 1862, according to the estimate of Indian agent Moses David, the Menominees turned out "not less than 45 tons of maple sugar, mostly of an excellent quality"; three-fourths of this amount was "disposed of to traders at an average of eight cents per pound" (RCIA 1862: 332). From a missionary perspective, the economic potential of maple sugar could serve to secure the Menominees' incorporation in a larger market economy without recourse to hunting or trapping—and thus provide a further stepping stone on their road to "civilization."

Gachet was busy with the pastoral care of a growing congregation and joyfully immersed in his diverse ethnographic and linguistic researches when in the spring of 1862 he received the order to leave Keshena and go to Patna to assist the aging Bishop Anastasius Hartmann. The news struck him "like a thunderbolt out of a clear sky." All of a sudden pulled away from a life and a purpose that for him "had held so many attractions," he left the mission "with a heavy heart. [...] Farewell, then, beautiful American soil. I had thought to have found on you my second home [...]" (Gachet 1890: 317, 321).

14 On Gachet's sojourn and work in India, see Rotzetter in this volume (esp. pp. 16–19).

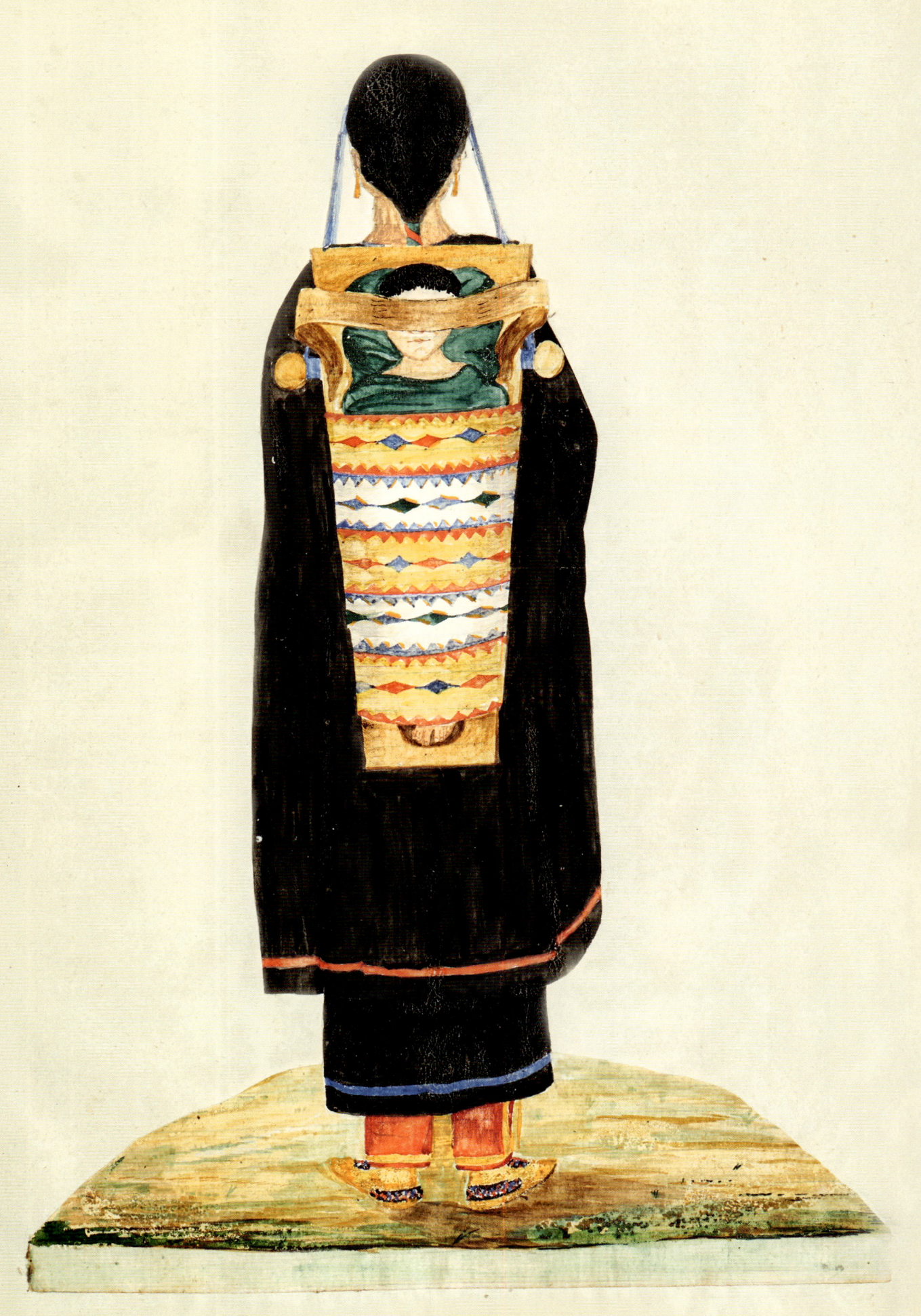

ANTOINE MARIE GACHET'S ETHNOGRAPHIC HERITAGE
Contextual and Comparative Notes

Fig. 31
Manner of Carrying a Child with a Burdenstrap.
Drawing by Antoine Marie Gachet ("American Diary," p. 287). Courtesy of the Capuchin Friary, Fribourg.

Depicted is the typical wooden cradleboard to which children were strapped for easy carrying, supported by a footrest and protected from accidental injury by a wooden bow over the head, to which a sunshade or toys could be attached. The image also documents the use of colorful cloth wrappers elaborately decorated with silk ribbon appliqué.

The ethnographic record left by Antoine Marie Gachet offers an intriguing glimpse of Menominee life around the mid-nineteenth century. It is a narrow and momentary glimpse for sure, but one that is exceptionally focused. The small collection of objects obtained within the first year of Gachet's brief sojourn on the Menominee Reservation is contextualized by the keen ethnographic observations he recorded in his diary (and edited for publication in his later life; cp. Gachet 1890), where he also described the circumstances of acquisition of at least some of the artifacts. His notes are furthermore accompanied by a series of naive but lovingly detailed drawings that visualize his impressions and experiences. Apart from exploring the objects' cultural use and significance, Gachet also endeavored to record their indigenous designations whenever possible—in keeping with his general linguistic ambitions, which culminated in the composition of a Menominee grammar (Favre 1954b, Gachet s.a., 1954). As such, the collection constitutes an important source for the historical ethnography of the western Great Lakes region and a valuable reference point for the comparative analysis of historically collected objects lacking attribution or recorded collection histories.

The Collection

In spite of this unusually comprehensive documentation, it is difficult to determine the exact contents of the original collection, of which less than thirty pieces appear to have survived. The inventory accompanying Gachet's donation to the Musée d'Antiquités of his native city of Fribourg has not been preserved. A letter by the director of the Ministry of Public Education to the guardian of the Capuchin Friary in Fribourg, dated 28 November 1860, acknowledges receipt of a shipment by "the Reverend Father A. Marie Gachet, missionary among the Menominees," containing "44 Indian articles for our museum," as well as a number of objects destined as gifts for various individuals: a [feather] fan "for his Eminence, the Bishop"; a birchbark roll and box filled with maple sugar for the Capuchin fathers; a pair of moccasins "for Comte de Diesbach"; a pair of moccasins "for Madame la Comtesse Fegely Maillardoz"; two small "cane baskets" for the Mother Superior of the Convent [of Montorge]; and a box of maple sugar for the donor's father.[1] The letter further states that all objects had been delivered to their proper recipients and that the museum would take care to honor the memory of Gachet's gift with labels mentioning the donor's name, the year of donation, and the origin of the artifacts (Direction de l'Instruction Publique 1860).[2]

Unfortunately, only a limited number of objects today still bear such labels identifying them beyond doubt as collected by Gachet (Fig. 32). The wording of these extant labels echoes Gachet's diction and they evidently reproduce information supplied by him, their consecutive numbering suggesting the sequence of an original inventory. Gaps in this sequence caused by the loss of labels and/or objects can be filled by recourse to typewritten lists of labels, produced at an unknown point in time, which likewise seem to go back to an original artifact list. These transcripts are close to but not always identical with the surviving object labels and in some cases are more detailed than the former. It is on the basis of these records—in concordance with the respective object entries of a 1940 typewritten inventory of the Fribourg collections and of a more recent card catalogue—that a reconstruction of Gachet's original inventory has been attempted (see pp. 83–87 below).[3] The resultant catalogue raisonné comprises thirty-three entries, several of which relate to more than one object. Whether all of the "44 Indian articles" of the donation are in fact covered by these entries cannot be determined conclusively. Many of the artifacts are missing today, and we also do not know how the specimens collectively subsumed under individual entries were actually counted when processed by the museum upon receipt.

At the same time, several undocumented Great Lakes objects in the Fribourg collection invite speculation as to their possible links to Gachet. None of them can directly be matched with entries in the transcript of labels of the 1860 donation, but it cannot be ruled out that these lists are incomplete. This conjecture is supported by Gachet's reference to a beaver(skin), given to him by the Saulteaux husband of a Menominee woman in his congregation, which he describes at length and claims to have donated to the museum of his native city (Gachet 1890: 241). This object has left no trace in the above-mentioned records but is listed in Grangier's historical review (1880–1881: 86) as part of the natural history department; unfortunately, it can no longer be located in the present collection of the Musée d'histoire naturelle Fribourg.[4] It is known that Gachet made a

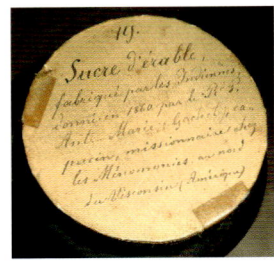

Fig. 32
Original label on a glass jar containing pieces of maple sugar (cat.no. 2031): "19. *Maple sugar, made by the Indian women, donated in 1860 by the Rev. Father Ant.-Marie (Gachet), Capuchin, missionary among the Ménomonies, in the north of Wisconsin (America).*"

[1] Etienne Marilley (1804–1889), Bishop of Lausanne and Geneva residing in Fribourg.

Comte Alphonse de Diesbach de Belleroche (1809–1888) was active in the promotion of agricultural and railroad interests in Fribourg.

Comtesse Marie Fégely Maillardoz (1820–1905) was the owner of a mansion in Monterschu in the parish of Gurmels (Cormondes), which she bequeathed to create an orphanage.

[2] The museum of the canton of Fribourg, founded in 1823 as a cabinet of natural history and physics, later included separate departments or "museums" of antiquities, ethnography, numismatics, etc. (Grangier 1880–1881). It was the ancestor of the present Musée d'histoire naturelle, whose ethnographic collections were transferred to the University of Fribourg in 1940.

[3] These data were first compiled by Christian Feest during a visit to the

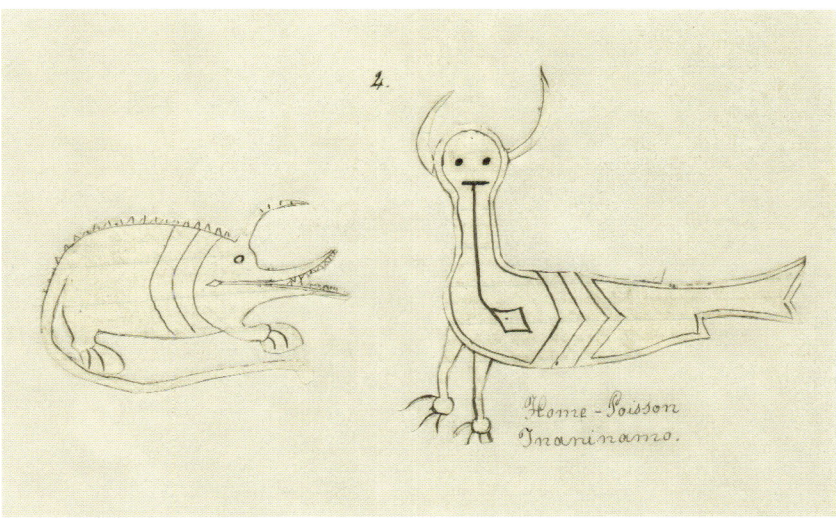
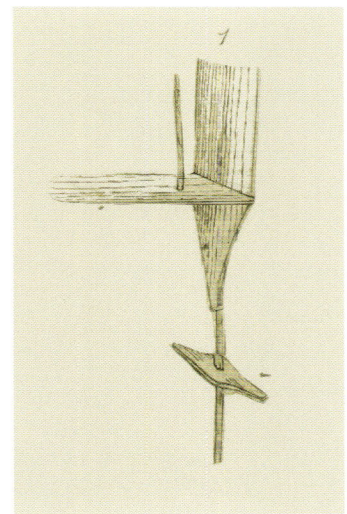

Figs. 33 and 34 Representations of the images on an engraved wooden board (p. 63, cat. no. 2036) and of the jacklight of a model dugout canoe (p. 67, cat.no. 2064) in the Gachet collection. Drawings by Antoine Marie Gachet ("American Diary," pp. 160 and 423). Courtesy of the Capuchin Friary, Fribourg.

Fribourg collections in 1986 and supplemented during a joint research visit with the present author in 1989 (cp. Kasprycki 2005: esp. 32–38). The collection was examined again in preparation of this catalogue in December 2015.

⁴ Peter Wandeler, Musée d'histoire naturelle Fribourg, pers. com., 29 January 2018.

⁵ Grangier's claim that all objects donated by Gachet came from the Menominees may be due to the ambiguity of the term "indien"; he also misdates the second donation to 1866, when Gachet was still in India.

second donation to the museum in 1868 shortly after his return from India, which apparently consisted of only a few objects, since Grangier (1880–1881: 80) refers to the total number of items received by the museum from Gachet as "about fifty." However, as stated in a letter by the Ministry of Public Education thanking Gachet for this gift (Direction de l'Instruction Publique 1868), these were artifacts he brought back from India (as yet not identified in the Fribourg collections), and it is unlikely that any further Native American objects were included in this donation.⁵ A more promising surmise with regard to the undocumented Great Lakes objects in question would be that some of the artifacts presented by Gachet as gifts to various individuals subsequently found their way into the museum, albeit without the information originally accompanying them. Four of these artifacts—three pairs of moccasins and the beaded lapels of a man's coat or shirt (cat.nos. 2004, 2005, 2006, and 2045ab)—were tentatively added to the catalogue raisonné (as items [30] to [33]) based on stylistic comparison and circumstantial evidence discussed in greater detail below (see pp. 78–82). A few other artifacts previously associated with Gachet were eliminated on the same grounds as most likely not collected by him: a sweetgrass tray (cat.no. 2011), a "curlicue" splint basket (cat.no. 2012), and a toboggan model (cat.no. 2067) are listed in the 1940 inventory as deriving from "Canada," the latter item also bearing an original label to this effect; a pair of miniature snowshoes (cat.no. 2038) and a souvenir wall-pocket made of a moose foot (cat.no. 2063) may have come from the same source. All of these objects appear to be of a somewhat later date.

Gachet's drawings of assorted Menominee artifacts, neatly labeled and arranged in tables, add a fascinating dimension to the collection, but in some respects raise more questions than they answer about missing objects or the ambiguous attribution of existing objects to Gachet's collecting activities. It is tempting at first glance to assume that these images depict artifacts he had

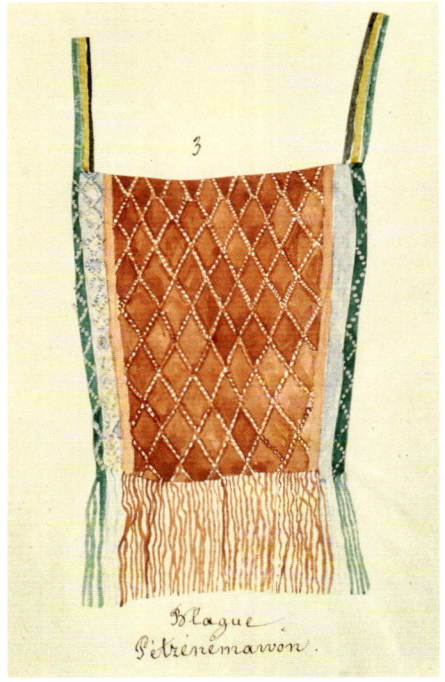 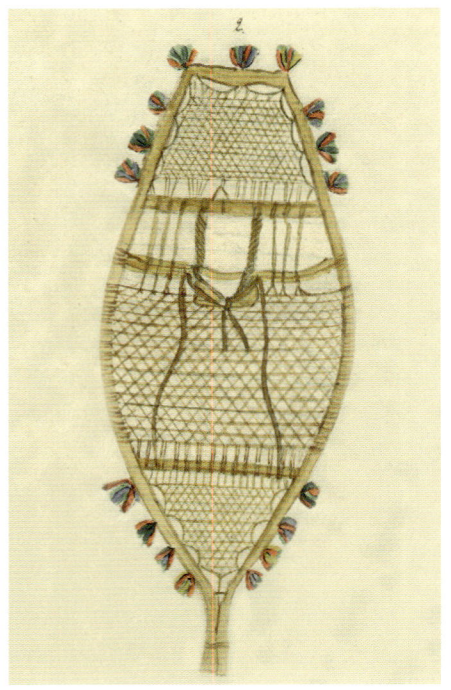

Figs. 35 and 36
Bag. Pétzénémawon (left) and *Snowshoe* (right). Drawings by Antoine Marie Gachet ("American Diary," pp. 383 and 347). Courtesy of the Capuchin Friary, Fribourg.

acquired for his collection, but this assumption is challenged upon closer inspection. While several of the drawings unmistakably match extant objects, some artistic license or shortcomings notwithstanding (e.g., Figs. 33, 34, 52, 54, 57), others deviate from the analogous pieces in the collection to such an extent as to suggest that similar but not identical objects are depicted (e.g., Figs. 58 and 59). These variant drawings bear up well to ethnographic scrutiny, but whether their real-life models were actually collected or whether they just reflect Gachet's detailed observations, is a question that remains unresolved. Indeed, it appears that Gachet illustrated some of these artifacts as "type specimens" much in the same way that he recorded samples of fauna and flora (cp. Figs. 9, 27, 46).

This may also hold true for a third group of object images, for which there are no corresponding artifacts in the collection today. The initial hope upon rediscovery of the drawings that they might illustrate the no longer extant objects of the original donation had to be quickly dismissed. In only one case can the representation of an artifact—a Chippewa pipestem decorated with bird skins (cp. Fig. 52 below)—be linked unequivocally to a now lost item documented in the records (catalogue raisonné no. 04)—an identification additionally supported by a reference to this pipe in Gachet's book (1890: 178). A tobacco bag of muskrat skin listed as part of the original collection (catalogue raisonné no. 05), on the other hand, is not the one illustrated by Gachet (cp. Fig. 54 below), which is specifically identified as a skunk-skin bag ("Shikak-Pétzénémawon"; cp. *seka·k*, 'skunk', Bloomfield 1975: 237; *pe'tcînamauan*, 'tobacco-bag', Skinner 1921: 365). Similar bags were used in the rituals of the Medicine Society—such

6 Similar bags were collected among the Chippewas since the 1830s (cp., e.g., Feest 1998: figs. 12, 13; Penney 1992: 78, #12; Feest and Kasprycki 1999: fig. 87; Flint Institute of Arts 1973: 55, #208). Somewhat later Menominee examples, featuring additional panels of appliqué beadwork, were acquired by Alanson Skinner for the American Museum of Natural History (e.g., cat.nos. 50/9854, 50.1/5900, 50.1/6632, 50.1/6633, 50.2/2467; cp. Skinner 1921: pl. CV). This is also the type of pouch worn by Menominee chief Souligny in Fig. 25 (see p. 32 above).

For Menominee snowshoes, see Hoffman 1896: 263–265; Skinner 1921: 212, pl. XLI; and a specimen in the Field Museum in Chicago (cat.no. 155.904, M. G. Chandler coll.).

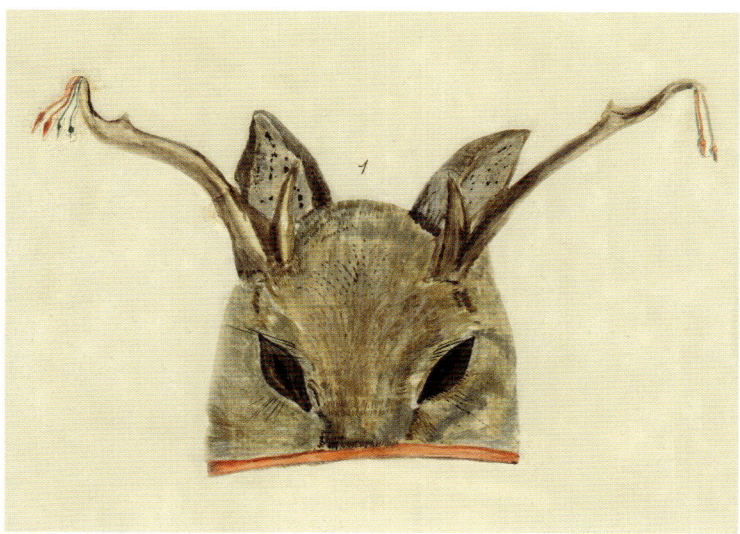
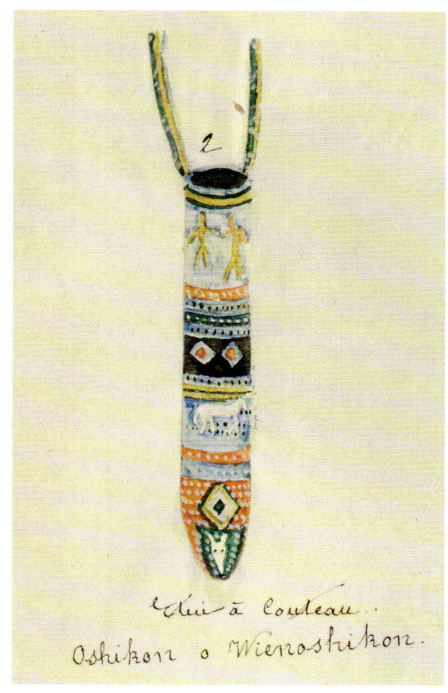

Figs. 37 and 38
Headdress of a Deer Head (left) and *Knifesheath. Oshikon o Wienoshikon* (right).
Drawings by Antoine Marie Gachet ("American Diary," pp. 347 and 383).
Courtesy of the Capuchin Friary, Fribourg.

[7] The only other horned headdress collected among the Menominees is a buffalo headdress in the American Museum of Natural History, said to have belonged to Chief Oshkosh (cat.no. 50.1/4364; cp. Skinner 1913: fig. 24).

[8] For comparative discussions of Menominee quillwork on knifecases and pouches, see, e.g., Feest and Kasprycki 2001, Kasprycki 2015. Feest (2002: 266) identifies Gachet as a major source on wearing knifecases around the neck.

as a skunk-skin pouch illustrated by Skinner (1920: pl. VII)—and apart from tobacco they probably contained various medicines and spiritually powerful objects. Whether the drawing of the skunk-skin pouch can therefore be related to the "bags of Indian amulets" mentioned in the transcript copies of original labels (catalogue raisonné no. 27) is likewise doubtful, since the French designation "sachets" may also indicate the various textile bags that were used for such purposes and are well known from the ethnographic record (e.g., Skinner 1913: fig. 25; Kasprycki 2006: 143–144, figs. 17, 18).

Irrespective of their limited usefulness for the identification of missing objects, Gachet's illustrations of artifacts provide valuable insights into Menominee material culture around the mid-nineteenth century. A fingerwoven shoulder bag made of wool yarn and glass beads (Fig. 35) and a snowshoe (Fig. 36) compare well with specimens known from various museum collections.[6] Of particular interest are his drawings of a deer headdress (Fig. 37) and a knifesheath (Fig. 38; "Oshikon o Wienoshikon"; cp. *a'sikun wiûna'kun*, 'knife-sheath', Skinner 1921: 141); both objects would constitute exceptional ethnographic examples had they been part of the collection and survived. Gachet noted that horned headdresses like this were worn by warriors during dances and ceremonies (Gachet 1890: 269–270).[7] The anthropomorphic and zoomorphic designs of the quill(?)-decorated knifecase are quite intriguing; they do not occur on any of the known Great Lakes examples, but are iconographically related to the various stylized representational designs found on quilled buckskin pouches from the region.[8]

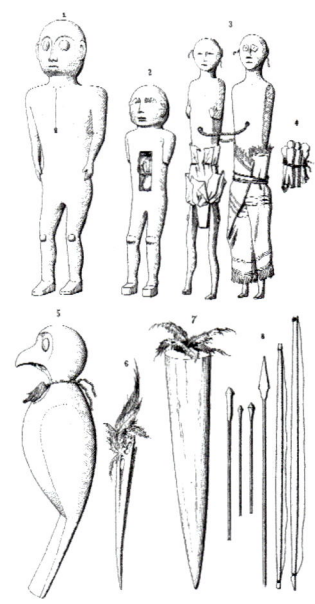
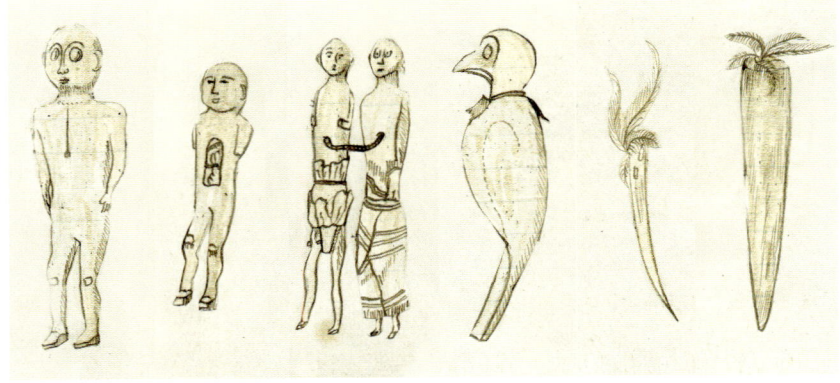

Fig. 39 (left)
Menominee ceremonial objects collected by the Belgian priest Florimond Bonduel around 1850. Lithograph (after Bonduel 1855: pl. opp. 7).
Fig. 40 (above)
Drawings made by Gachet after Bonduel's plate ("American Diary," p. 135).
Courtesy of the Capuchin Friary, Fribourg.

Gachet's endeavor to collect and record Menominee material culture in a scholarly fashion preceded the concerted efforts of the newly established discipline of anthropology by a few decades, even though Menominee artifacts had found their way into European and Euroamerican collections more or less accidentally and more or less well documented since at least the late eighteenth century.[9] His ambition stands in a tradition of missionary collecting activities among the Menominees and their neighbors that had started three decades earlier with the onset of sustained Catholic missionization in the western Great Lakes region. A significant role in the early traffic of Native objects from various mission posts to European collections and museums seems to have been played by the German-born priest Friedrich Rese,[10] vicar general of the diocese of Cincinnati and from 1833 first bishop of Detroit. In 1829 Rese had helped to launch the Leopoldine Foundation in Vienna, a charitable organization that came to provide funds, equipment, and personnel for the North American missions throughout the nineteenth century (Kummer 1966). Contemplating the establishment of an "Indian museum," Rese encouraged the missionaries under his jurisdiction not only to study the indigenous languages but also to collect objects of Native manufacture (Rese 1830), some of which found their way to Europe through the channels of the Leopoldine Foundation. Rese thus acquired (or mediated the acquisition) around 1830 of some of the earliest documented Menominee artifacts, which eventually became part of the private collection of Johann Georg Schwarz and are preserved in the Weltmuseum Wien (Kasprycki 2007).

Rese may not have instigated but perhaps advocated the ethnographic collection of the Slovenian pioneer missionary Friedrich Baraga, who had been

[9] Significant early nineteenth-century Menominee objects can be found, e.g., in the Wisconsin Historical Museum, Madison, WI; the Neville Public Museum, Green Bay, WI; the Weltkulturen Museum in Frankfurt, Germany; or the Weltmuseum Wien, Austria.

[10] Rese later came to spell his last name as Résé or Rézé in order to ensure its correct pronunciation in English.

reluctant at first when requested in 1833 by the Carniolian Provincial Museum in Ljubljana to collect for the newly founded institution and had pleaded pastoral duties as an excuse. However, three years later and probably occasioned by a fund-raising trip to Europe, Baraga donated a number of Ottawa and Chippewa objects gathered in Michigan and Wisconsin to the precursor of todays' Slovenian Ethnographic Museum. This museum also holds ethnographic artifacts acquired by Baraga's fellow missionaries and countrymen Franz Pierz and Ivan Čebul, who had followed in his footsteps and eventually came to work at several of Baraga's earlier mission posts (cp. Golob 1997, Feest 1998, Kasprycki 1998).

Around the same time, the French association L'Œuvre de la Propagation de la Foi, founded in Lyon in 1822 and model for the Leopoldine Foundation, likewise received ethnographic objects from missionaries active in the western Great Lakes area, among them the Redemptorist fathers who had alternately overseen the Ottawa and Menominee missions in the 1830s. These materials, which have received little scholarly attention as yet, are currently held by the Musée des Confluences in Lyon.[11]

Martin Pitzer's much better known collection of Ottawa artifacts in the Weltmuseum Wien likewise derived from a missionary context. In 1851 the church painter from Salzburg, Austria, followed an invitation by Franz Pierz to visit the Ottawa missions of Lacroix (Cross Village) and Arbre Croche (Harbor Springs) in Michigan in order to embellish the Native churches. Pitzer later toured the objects he had acquired in a traveling exhibition intended to raise money for the missions and published a small catalogue, to which Friedrich Baraga contributed the artifacts' Ottawa designations (Pitzer 1854).[12]

The Belgian priest Florimond Bonduel, one of Gachet's predecessors among the Menominees, pursued similar goals when he presented a number of Menominee ceremonial objects to his audiences during a lecture tour in Europe in 1855. He subsequently donated the artifacts to the Museo Borgiano di Propaganda Fide in Rome, which was incorporated by the Museo Missionario Etnologico (of the Vatican Museums) in 1926. Most of these objects and their documentation were lost over time; a few remaining pieces could be identified on the basis of the illustrations and corresponding descriptions in a pamphlet published by Bonduel in 1855 (Fig. 39).[13]

All these collections provide insights not only into the material culture of the closely related Algonquian groups of the western Great Lakes region, but also into missionary attitudes toward the material manifestations of indigenous customs and beliefs. As such, they furnish the backdrop against which to judge the merits of Gachet's choices as a collector. Given his early interest in missionary work and his wide reading in various languages, he was probably aware of his predecessors' efforts at collecting, even though he could hardly have been

[11] For illustrations of some of these objects, see Feest 2008a: 244, 246; Kasprycki 2008: 71, 73. Cp. also http://www.museedesconfluences.fr/fr/ressources/collection-de-l%C5%93uvre-de-la-propagation-de-la-foi.

[12] For objects in the Pitzer collection, see Feest 1968: pls. 5–7, 9c; Graham 1983, 1984; Feest and Kasprycki 1993: 60, 64, 66, 68, 70; Phillips 1998: 159, 180, 181; Kasprycki 2008: 74, 75.

[13] Three engraved wooden "song boards" (cat.nos. Am 3231, Am 3226A, Am 3227) and three birchbark strips with pictographic records (cat.nos. Am 3226B, Am 3226C, Am 3226D) are known to have survived (cp. Kasprycki 2008: 78, 82–83).

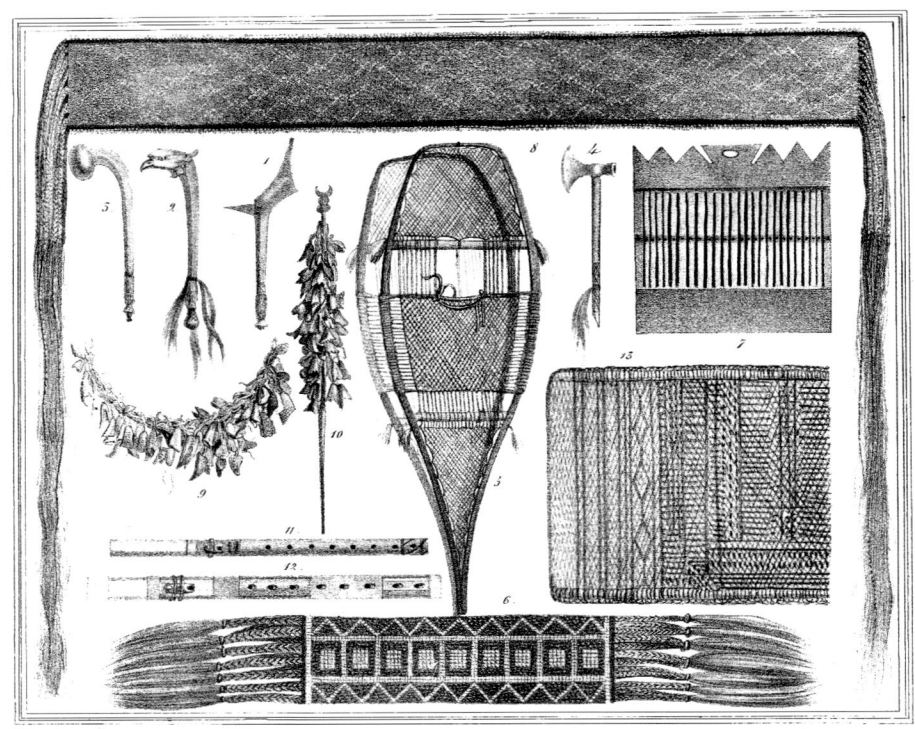

Fig. 41
Bracelets, Mats, Weapons, Snowshoes and Musical Instruments of the North American Indians. Lithograph (after Castelnau 1842: pl. XXXII).

Apart from the "belt of an Iroquois chief" (no. 8), provenances are provided for two other objects illustrated in this plate: a wooden heddle (no. 7) "with which the women of the Folle-Avoines [Menominees] are weaving wool" and a Menominee rush mat (no. 13).

familiar with the objects assembled in previous decades. He admired Baraga's missionary achievements and used the latter's linguistic works to learn the Ojibwa language when preparing for his own mission. Baraga's ethnographic treatise (1837), which also contains a few references to objects he collected, may have served as an inspiration as well. Parallels can indeed be drawn between Gachet's *Cinq Ans en Amérique* and Baraga's earlier publication: While more ambitious in his scholarly orientation and breadth, Gachet followed his role model in the attempt to present his personal observations within in a more general and comparative cultural history of American Indians.

There is considerable overlap as well in the composition of the two collections: Each contains a variety of pipestems, a ball-headed club, carved wooden spoons (in Gachet's case only one), a miniature bark canoe, several quill-decorated birchbark objects including maple sugar "mococks" and a feather fan with birchbark handle (the example in Gachet's collection no longer extant), and several pairs of moccasins. The snowshoes, fingerwoven shoulder bag, cradleboard, and cradle wrapper acquired by Baraga are missing in Gachet's collection but were drawn by him in minute detail (cp. Figs. 31, 35, 36). The game of lacrosse, represented in Gachet's collection by a lacrosse stick and ball, on the other hand, is not even mentioned in Baraga's book. With the exception of musical instruments, the two missionaries' choices of objects also closely resemble the array of "typical" Native artifacts deemed collectibles by the French traveler

[14] In contrast to the somewhat simplistic scenic views and portraits in Castelnau's travel account, which may go back to his own sketches (cp. Fig. 13 above), the tables of objects are executed in exquisite detail. It seems safe to assume that artifacts brought back to France served as props for the lithographer. Unfortunately, the fate of this collection is unknown.

[15] One of the earliest documented examples is the so-called "Rankin costume." Consisting of a blanket, skirt, and leggings and said to have been worn by Sophia Theresa Rankin, the granddaughter of a Menominee/Ottawa chief, with Louis Grignon in 1802, it is today preserved in the Neville Public Museum (cat.no. 70/1948; Feder 1965: back cover).

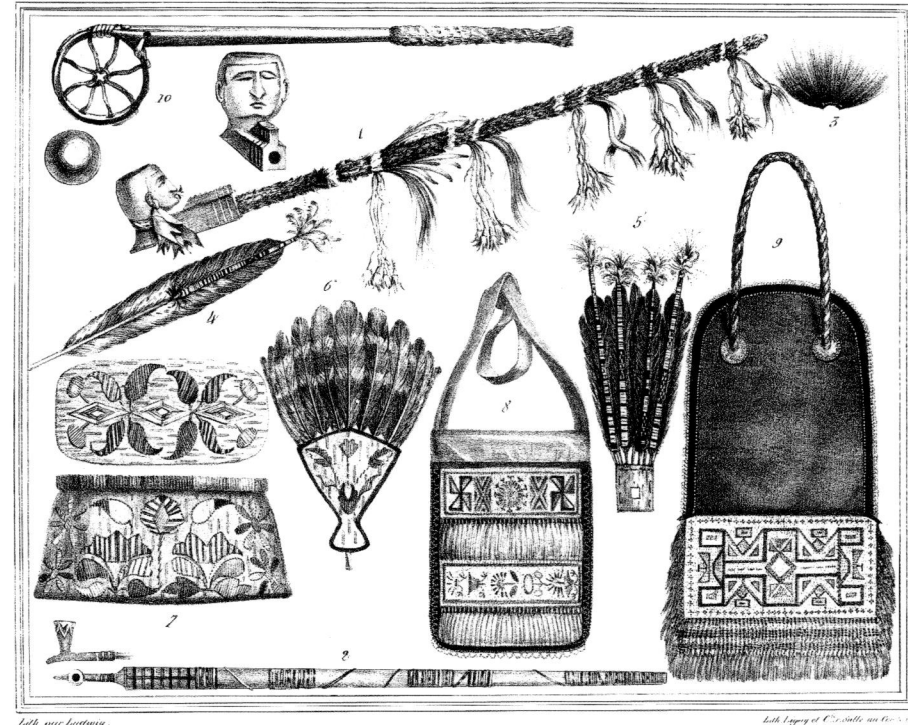

Fig. 42
Ornaments, Calumets, Boxes, etc. of the Indians of North America.
Lithograph (after Castelnau 1842: pl. XXXIII).

No specific attributions are given for the lidded birchbark box decorated with porcupine quills (no. 7) and the feather fan with birchbark handle (no. 6), which were typical commodities produced by Ottawa, Chippewa, and Menominee women for the souvenir trade in the western Great Lakes area.

[16] Only a few similar pieces have survived in museums. Two of them were collected by Walter C. Wyman around 1900 (Ethnologisches Museum, Berlin, cat.no. IV B 7611, "Ojibwa"; Wisconsin History Museum, cat.no. 1954.1621, "Menominee").

[17] Early examples made of white "pony" beads and featuring motifs in a contrasting dark color (e.g., Thunderbirds on a Menominee pair in the Neville Public Museum, cat.no. 445/3329; cp. Feder 1965: no. 31) were later replaced by polychrome garters in a variety of geometric and stylized floral designs (the Charles Edwin Kelsey collection in the Wisconsin History Museum, e.g., contains numerous examples obtained on the Menominee Reservation between 1887 and 1895.)

Francis de Castelnau, who toured the Great Lakes region in 1838 (Castelnau 1842: pls. XXXII, XXXIII; cp. Figs. 41, 42).[14]

The comparative lack of textile arts in Gachet's collection, restricted to several beaded dress items, is a little surprising in view of the ample pictorial documentation provided by his drawings. Menominee silk ribbon appliqué on blankets, skirts, and leggings of wool fabric,[15] of which there are several superb specimens in the Schwarz/Rese collection in Vienna (Kasprycki 2007: figs. 10–14), may have been on the decline by Gachet's time, even though his illustration of a cradle wrapper (Fig. 31) nicely compares with the piece collected by Baraga three decades earlier (Golob 1997: 133, no. 55; cp. Feest 1998: 296–298).[16] Finger-woven belts or shoulder bags, however, would certainly have been available, and heddle-woven garters of glass beads like the one illustrated by Castelnau (Fig. 41: no. 6) were becoming ever more fashionable in the later decades of the nineteenth century.[17] Conspicuous is the absence of woven rush mats, which were not only ubiquitous household items serving as carpets, wall hangings, and bed sheets but were also highly valued trade goods and played a prominent role in ritual gift giving. Western commentators had appreciated their intricate designs and color schemes since the seventeenth century (Kinietz 1965: 244; Castelnau 1842: 95; Kohl 1859, 1: 17–18), and mats had become collector's items since at least the early 1800s (Schoolcraft 1821: pl. ii; cp. Fig. 41: no. 13). Like other missionaries before and after him, Gachet joined in the praise of the technical skills and aesthetic accomplishments of Menominee mat weavers, regarding their products "worthy of European parlors," and he also illustrated the use of rush mats in various contexts (Gachet 1890: 251, 262, 399; cp. Figs. 10, 19, 51).

Gachet was clearly interested in the material expressions of Menominee religion—objects that had always been a primary focus of missionary interventions—and paid special attention to their religious paraphernalia in his account of traditional beliefs and ceremonial practices (e.g., Gachet 1890: 174–194, 244, 277, 279, 284–285). However, only very few objects were eventually chosen to supplement his collection: a wooden board engraved with the images of supernatural beings (cat.no. 2036) and now lost "bags of Indian amulets" (catalogue raisonné no. 27). Gachet's careful selection of artifacts differs markedly from the collection of his missionary predecessor, Florimond Bonduel, which was not so much the result of deliberate choice, but a more or less haphazard conglomeration of ceremonial objects surrendered to him by his converts before baptism. Gachet was well aware of his precursor's work, whom he also met in person during a visit to Green Bay in 1859 (Gachet 1890: 143). Having studied Bonduel's publication (1855) in minute detail (cp. Figs. 39 and 40), he devoted several pages in his own book to a critical revision of some of Bonduel's misguided conclusions, especially with regard to the interpretations of the engravings on a wooden board comparable to the one collected by himself. In stark contrast to Gachet's genuine and broad ethnographic interest, Bonduel simply regarded these objects as "glorious trophies" of Christianity's victory over "heathen darkness"—and implicitly of his own missionary success (Bonduel 1855: 6)—and his explanations were meant to emphasize this message. Gachet proved to be the superior ethnographer, willing to probe more deeply into Native mythology and beliefs in an attempt to understand the very religious practices he had set out to reform (Gachet 1890: 175–176, 210–216; Kasprycki 1994).

This is not to deny the fact that Gachet's pursuits were ultimately grounded both in the religious bias of his profession and in his conviction of the cultural

Fig. 43 (left)
Pagan Cemetery.
Drawing by Antoine Marie Gachet ("American Diary," p. 160). Courtesy of the Capuchin Friary, Fribourg.

Fig. 44 (right)
Wooden grave house in front of several rectangular bark dwellings.
Photograph (after Hoffman 1896: pl. XVIII).

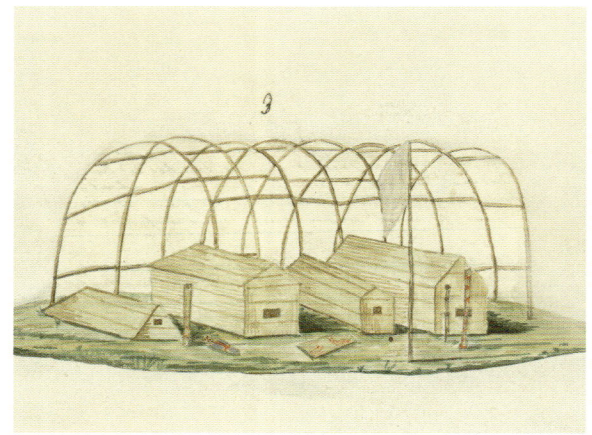

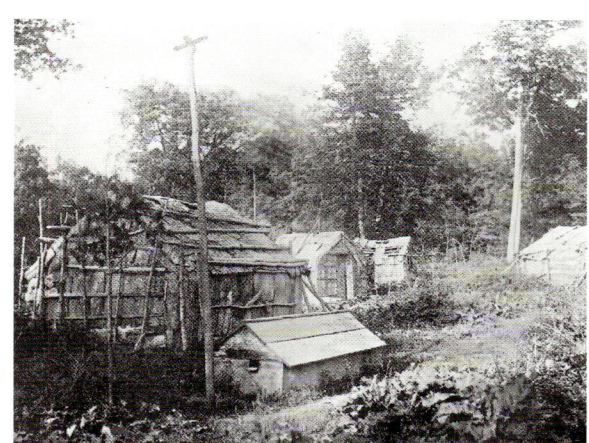

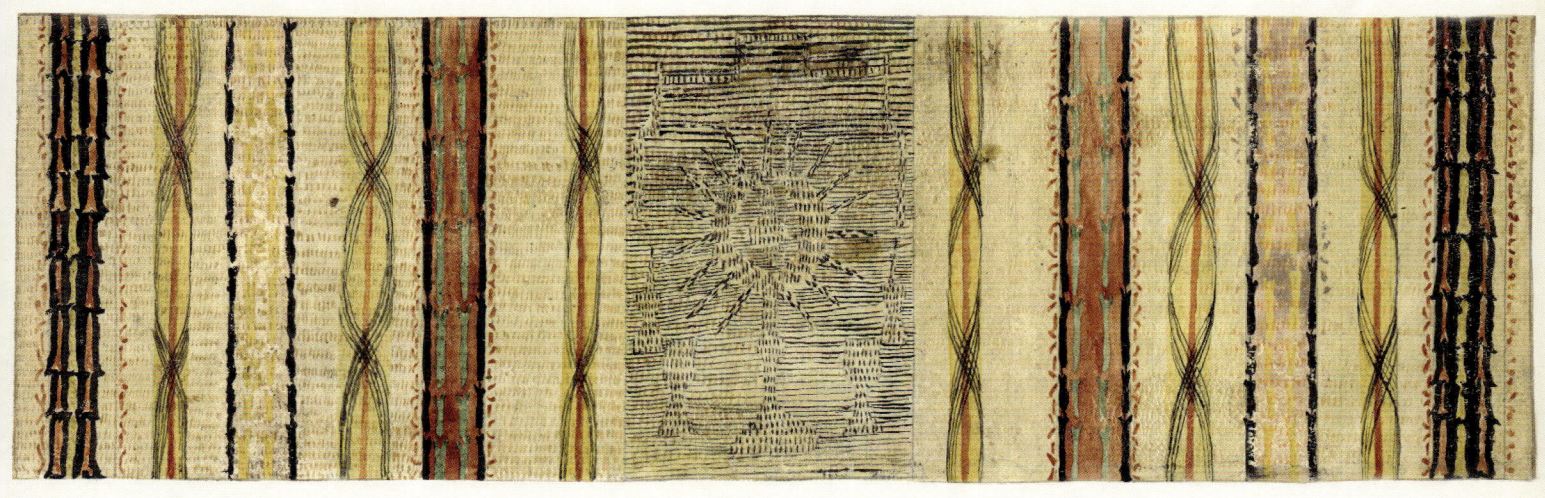

Fig. 45
Mat for the Great Altar.
Drawing by Antoine Marie
Gachet ("American Diary,"
p. 324). Courtesy of the
Capuchin Friary, Fribourg.

"Christian women brought
me beautiful mats, made
with their hands, to cover
the steps of the altar. They
excel in this branch of textile art. ... They know how
to weave into the fabric a
great variety of figures
without missing the pro-
portions. On one of these
mats, four meters long,
were crosses and stars, and
on another one a mon-
strance between candle-
sticks and flowerpots"
(Gachet 1890: 251).

superiority of Western civilization, which he shared with his Euroamerican contemporaries. While driven by sincere curiosity and scholarly ambition in the documentation of cultural phenomena, his judgements necessarily remained con-
strained by his missionary agenda, especially with regard to Menominee religious
ideas. He was tolerant of certain aspects of Native beliefs in which he thought to
discern incipient notions of Christian truths, but found strong words of disap-
proval for practices he considered incompatible with Christian morals and "civilization." His comments on Menominee religious paraphernalia ranged from
mild amusement over "curious superstitions" to outright rejection, and the medicine bags he kept for his collection were only part of the "shiploads" of such
objects committed to missionary bonfires that kept burning throughout the nineteenth century (Gachet 1890: 244, 284–285; Kasprycki 2006: 140–143). He
had no qualms taking the wooden board from a Menominee grave (Fig. 43), and
when the occasion presented itself, did not hesitate to destroy the material bases
of "pagan rites" just as his predecessors had done, reporting with satisfaction the
uprooting of the structure of a Menominee shaking tent during one of his walks
along the Wolf River (Gachet 1890: 233; cp. Fig. 22 above).

The prominent role played by the material manifestations of indigenous
beliefs in missionary discourse was matched by the importance attached to the
materiality of Catholic religion, to which missionaries attributed considerable
"power of persuasion": "The Indian cannot live of ideas alone," Gachet was convinced, "he needs a religion whose cult speaks to his eyes as well as to his heart"
1890: 264–265). In the absence of funds and supplies for the equipment of the
churches, recourse was often taken to indigenous manufactures. The resultant
material culture of Native Christianity, outwardly combining new forms with
local materials and techniques, occasionally also blended novel and traditional

ideas and thus reflected the gradual incorporation of Christian doctrines into Native epistemological systems (Fig. 45; Kasprycki 2006: 146–168). Most often these objects were considered provisionary solutions, to be replaced as soon as products of Euroamerican fabrication became available, and only a small number of them have been preserved. Significantly, the famous altar ensemble of quill-decorated birchbark used in the Ottawa church of Cross Village, Michigan, could only be acquired by the church painter Martin Pitzer because it was substituted at the time with a new altar made in Detroit, to the embellishment of which Pitzer lent his artistic talents (Pitzer 1854: 11).[18] No comparable Menominee objects were ever collected, even though the use of birchbark candle sticks and containers is also documented for the Menominee mission. The Italian priest Samuele Mazzuchelli, for instance, is known to have sent a birchbark box made to hold communion wafers as a present to Pope Gregory XVI in 1832 (Alderson and Alderson 1974: [28]).[19] Gachet, who described in detail his congregation's efforts to adorn the church and to provide the material requirements for the various religious celebrations in the Catholic ritual calendar, unfortunately did not care to collect any of these artifacts.

The absence of rush mats in Gachet's collection mentioned above is all the more surprising in view of the fact that they constituted a standard feature in the furnishing of the churches, the finest pieces being reserved as altar cloths or antependiums (cp. Fig. 10 above; Gachet 1890: 251). While simple household mats usually featured a variety of striped designs, other mats with more complex geometric or figurative patterns are known to have been used in ceremonial contexts, most notably as wrappings of sacred bundles, and often depicted supernatural beings.[20] Their transfer to the novel ritual setting of the Catholic mass may have seemed a logical step to the Native converts, as is demonstrated by the altar mat in Pitzer's collection, whose images of Thunderbirds most probably escaped the missionaries' notice (Pitzer 1854: 12).[21] Growing familiarity with Catholic religious concepts apparently induced the gradual incorporation of Christian imagery into the inventory of weaving designs: The mat illustrated by Gachet quite spectacularly documents this iconographic shift from the representation of traditional sacred images to that of Christian motifs, in this case a monstrance (Fig. 45; Gachet 1890: 250; cp. Kasprycki 1996: 47–49). It is to be regretted that Gachet did not choose to include this fascinating object in his collection.

Gachet's Drawings and Ethnographic Writings

Cinq Ans en Amérique was apparently written by Gachet in the late 1870s or early 1880s in preparation of its publication in the *Revue de la Suisse Catholique* (1882–1890). This time frame is also supported by his copies on page 264 of the "American Diary" of two portraits of Conibo Indians from the Ucayali River (Peru)

[18] Apart from the "altar," consisting of a tabernacle and a set of six candle sticks, Pitzer's collection also contains two holy water containers of quill-decorated birchbark (Graham 1983: 24–25; Harrison et al. 1987: 69, no. W148; Feest and Kasprycki 1993: 70, no. 55; Kasprycki 2008: 66, 79).

[19] This may have been comparable to a birchbark case for communion wafers made by Christian Ottawas around 1840 and today held by the Musée des Confluences in Lyon (Feest 2008a: 246, 247).

[20] An interesting group of Menominee rush mats of unknown age is held by the Denver Art Museum (cat.nos. 1939.435–1939.446; Mrs. Orrin Brown collection); two of these mats exhibit the complex central design panels that impress the viewer with their subtle interplay of positive and negative forms (Whiteford and Rogers 1994: fig. 11). Walter J. Hoffman's collection at the National Museum of Natural History in Washington, DC, likewise contains a few Menominee rush mats (e.g., cat.nos. 135.831, 135.832). Mats acquired by Alanson B. Skinner are preserved at the American Museum of Natural History (Whiteford and Rogers 1994: fig. 7) and the Canadian Museum of History (cat.no. II-N-4; cp. Skinner 1921: 238–243).

[21] This well-known artifact was repeatedly exhibited and illustrated (e.g., Harrison et al. 1987: #W144; Kasprycki 2008: 79).

Fig. 46
Plants and Flowers of the Menominee Reservation [pl. 8].
Drawing by Antoine Marie Gachet ("American Diary," p. 261).
Courtesy of the Capuchin Friary, Fribourg.

45. *Small flowers, in groups, red and blue, mixed with white, single stem, blooming in August, which the Menominees call Shikénasha. The deer dig up the root or tuber to eat it. Crushed, this root serves as a plaster to cure nails. The same plaster, mixed with vinegar, is good against the bites of the rattlesnake.*
46. *Flowers with 5 petals.*
47. *Yellow flowers, in clusters, blooming in great numbers in August.*
48. *Shrub, with lilac-based, pendant flowers, with woody stem.*
49. *The white flowers of this plant spread out from their stem in the form of a sword. The root, of a very bitter taste, has a particularly purgative effect. The Indians make great use of it. They call it Shaposhihon Wishékaship.*
52. *A kind of potato, eaten by the Indians and called Matze-towok-paniok (Indian potato). After boiling the root, they are cooked again in maple sap, until the whole is reduced to a syrup of a certain thickness.*

Gachet's ten plates of plant illustrations document his interest in botany. Most of the plants for which he supplies details about their use by the Menominees were not included in Huron H. Smith's *Ethnobotany of the Menomini Indians* (1923); the exception here is no. 52: Groundnut (*Apios tuberosa* Moench.), "ma'tcetaupä'niûk" [Indian potatoes] (Smith 1923: 68–69, pl. XXIX, fig. 31, pl. XXX, fig. 1); pe'koutc, or ma'tcetauopin, wild or Indian potato (Skinner 1921: 152).

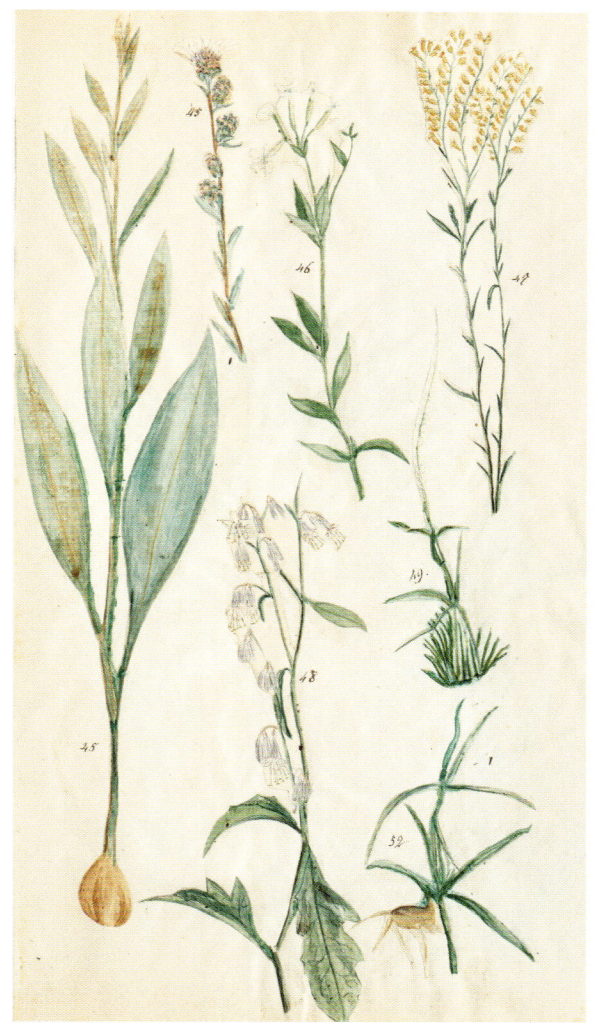

after Marcoy (1875, 1: 22–23). Parts of the text must have been based on an original diary, apparently now lost, and perhaps other notes. The images relating to the Menominees, executed in watercolors and pencil, were originally drawn on lined paper and later cut out and pasted on plates inserted at the appropriate places in the manuscript. While they are undated, this rearrangement of the images for the planned publication and above all their intricate ethnographic details strongly suggest that they were produced in the field.

Of the 43 plates, two are maps (cp. Figs. 1 and 14 above), while ten are devoted to the illustration of plants on the Menominee Reservation, accompanied by a descriptive list (Fig. 46). The remaining 31 plates with ethnographic subject matter are composed of 28 scenes and portraits and 22 artifacts (exclusive of the altogether eight drawings Gachet copied from Bonduel; cp. Fig. 40). In addition to the inscriptions on some of the drawings, there is also an incomplete list of illustrations attached to the "American Diary," which forms the basis for the captions used in this book.

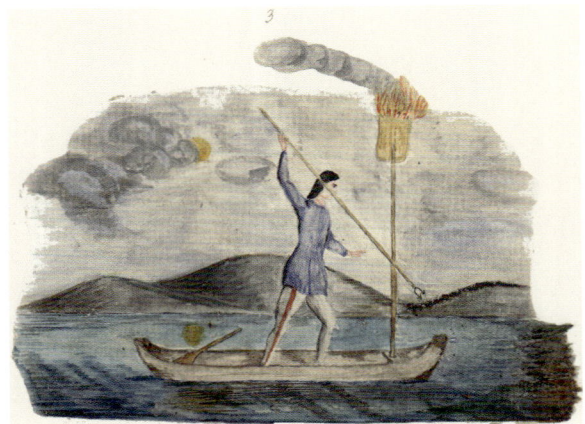

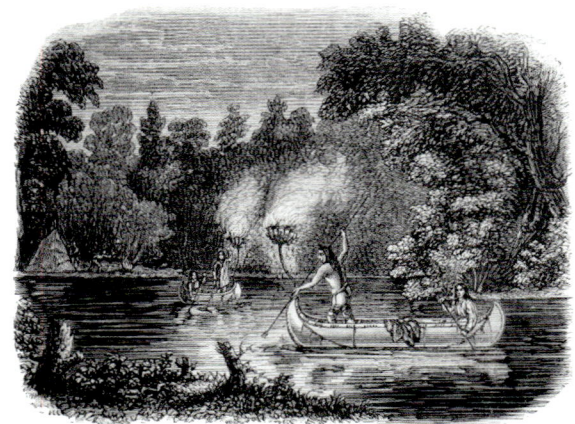

When compared with the corpus of Menominee images produced between 1825 and 1860 (Kasprycki 1990a), Gachet's drawings stand out with their scenic representations of subsistence activities and other aspects of Menominee daily life only rarely depicted by other artists,[22] as well as by the attention paid to the practice of Menominee Catholicism disregarded by others as "untraditional." All these images, while perhaps lacking artistic refinement, are rich in carefully observed ethnographic details. This is also true for Gachet's Menominee portraits, which however do not depict named individuals but rather "types" (e.g., "Indian war chief" or "Christian Menominee woman"; cp. Figs. 17, 18, 51)—in contrast to the major bulk of existing pictorial records that are made up of portraits of identified individuals. Gachet's artifact plates are exceptional: apart from Castelnau (Fig. 41), no other artist produced illustrations of specified Menominee artifacts.

In a long line of Catholic missionaries among the Menominees Gachet was the first who learned their language rather than relying on the related Ojibwa in his pastoral work (Gachet 1890: 280). He was also the first—after the physician and naturalist Edwin James a generation before him (Kasprycki 1990b)—to leave a substantial written record of the Menominee language, yet his achievements have remained almost unexplored. His Menominee grammar (Gachet s.a., 1954), inspired by Baraga's Ojibwa grammar (1850), was published in microform in 1954 with an essay by Blaise Favre (1954b), but only after the publication of Leonard Bloomfield's masterful *Menomini Language* (1962) and *Menominee Lexicon* (1975) was it briefly noted in Algonquianist studies by Miner (1977). His unfinished Menominee catechism (1862a) may have been based on an Ottawa catechism (Baraga 1858), of which Gachet owned a copy. His principal Menominee collaborator on his linguistic projects appears to have been Metz-Kinew (Big Eagle) (Gachet 1890: 232–233).

Gachet's contributions to Menominee ethnography have likewise been largely neglected. *Cinq Ans en Amérique*, originally published in a Swiss Catholic

Fig. 47 (left)
[Spearing fish at night].
Drawing by Antoine Marie Gachet ("American Diary," p. 423). Courtesy of the Capuchin Friary, Fribourg.

Fig. 48 (right)
Spearing by Torch-light on Fox River.
Engraving (after Paul Kane 1859: 31, no. 4).

While Gachet depicts the wooden "jacklights" of which he also collected a model (cat.no. 2064, see pp. 66–67), Paul Kane's rendering of the picturesque scenery shows the use of iron frames for the same purpose and may have been influenced by his boyhood memories of similar scenes about the Bay of Toronto (Kane 1859: 30–32).

[22] Apart from Castelnau's sketches of a Menominee village (Fig. 13 above) and a war dance (1842: pl. XVII) and Paul Kane's oil versions of Menominees *Fishing by Torchlight* (Harper 1971: 179, fig. 41, 277), all publicized in print (Fig. 48), there is a pencil sketch of a Menominee

cemetery by the Austrian artist Franz Hölzlhuber from the late 1850s preserved in the Glenbow Museum in Calgary, Alberta, which is comparable to similar depictions by Gachet (Kasprycki 1990a: fig. 71).

Fig. 49 (left)
Sacrifice of a Dog.
Drawing by Antoine Marie Gachet ("American Diary," p. 217). Courtesy of the Capuchin Friary, Fribourg.

"Near the lodge I noticed a post bearing the carved figure of a man's head and the body of a black dog with a bag of tobacco suspended from the neck. It was a sacrifice that had been offered for healing the sick" (Gachet 1890: 277).

Fig. 50 (right)
Muskrat Hunt.
Drawing by Antoine Marie Gachet ("American Diary," p. 443). Courtesy of the Capuchin Friary, Fribourg.

journal and subsequently as a book in a small number of copies, never reached an anthropological readership. An (at times faulty) English translation of an extract of the book (Bittle 1934–1935) almost completely disregarded its ethnographic contents. Nevertheless, together with the earlier account by the Indian agent C. C. Trowbridge (1823), Gachet's observations are the key sources on Menominee ethnography prior to the ethnographic fieldwork by Walter J. Hoffman and Alanson Skinner (see the bibliography at the end of the volume).

The two pre-anthropological studies differ significantly in their methodology and results but complement one another. Trowbridge's work was based on a questionnaire prepared by Lewis Cass, the Governor of Michigan Territory (Hallowell 1960: 40–41), which provided a systematic approach resulting in a focused presentation reminiscent of later professional ethnography—except for its neglect of material culture, in which Cass was not interested. By comparison, Gachet's ethnography at first glance seems old-fashioned and is rooted in the apodemic literature of the Renaissance, which was based on the complementary nature of *historia* (empirical facts) and *scientia* (systematic knowledge) (cp. Feest 2008b: 19–20). Thus, Gachet's book consists of a chronological narrative interspersed with "notices" summarizing selected subject matter (such as religion) in a coherent manner. While Trowbridge's sources of information remain anonymous and were probably all male, Gachet's narrative permits the reader to look at the dialogical process by which the data were obtained in his interaction with male and female (mostly Christian) Menominees.

As an ethnographer at the very least, Gachet clearly surpassed his role model Baraga. Together with his collection and drawings, presented here for the first time, his writings offer an unusually rich body of data providing insight into Menominee culture at a time of profound change and adaptation—reflecting the influences not only of Euroamerican culture but also of intense intertribal exchange, documenting continuities and changes in their material culture, and highlighting the dynamics of the cultural dialogue between the Menominees and the agents of Christianity.

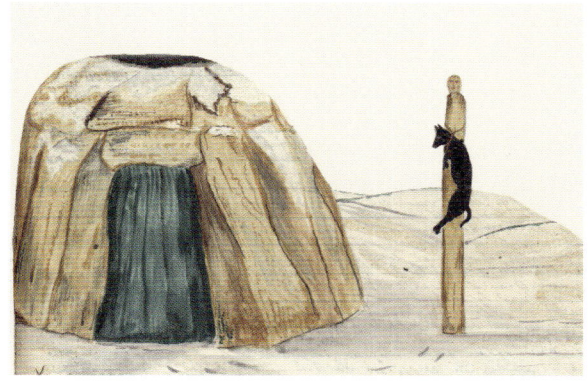
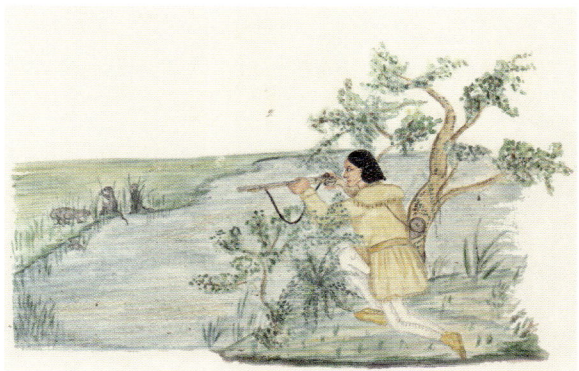

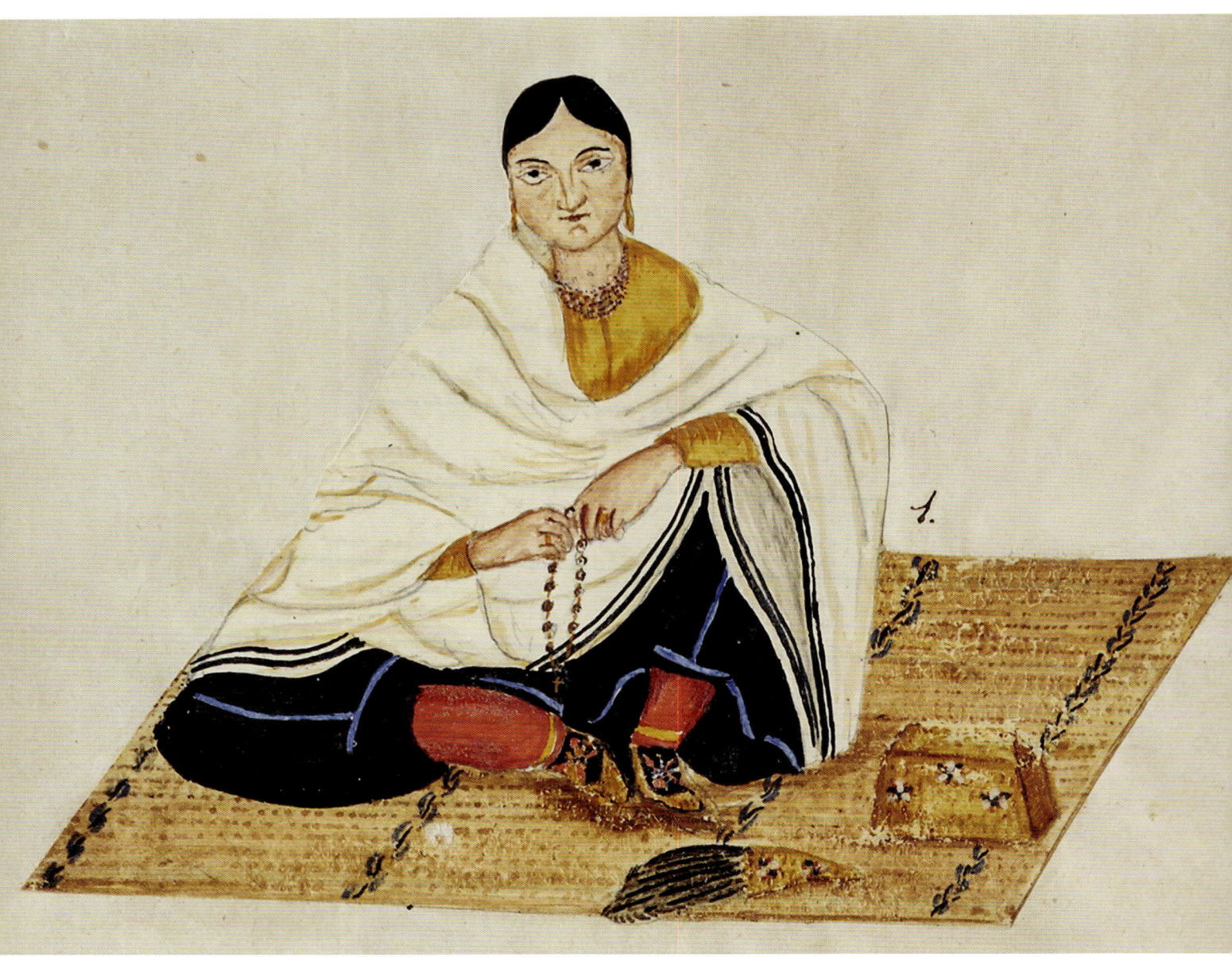

Fig. 51
Christian Menominee Woman Reciting the Rosary.
Drawing by Antoine Marie Gachet ("American Diary," p. 180). Courtesy of the Capuchin Friary, Fribourg.

Wrapped in a blanket and dressed in a blouse, skirt and leggings edged with silk ribbons, and beaded moccasins, the woman sitting on a rush mat is absorbed in her prayers. A birchbark box and feather fan decorated with porcupine quills placed at her side may be the product of her own hands.

ANTOINE MARIE GACHET'S
ETHNOGRAPHIC COLLECTION
With a Catalogue Raisonné

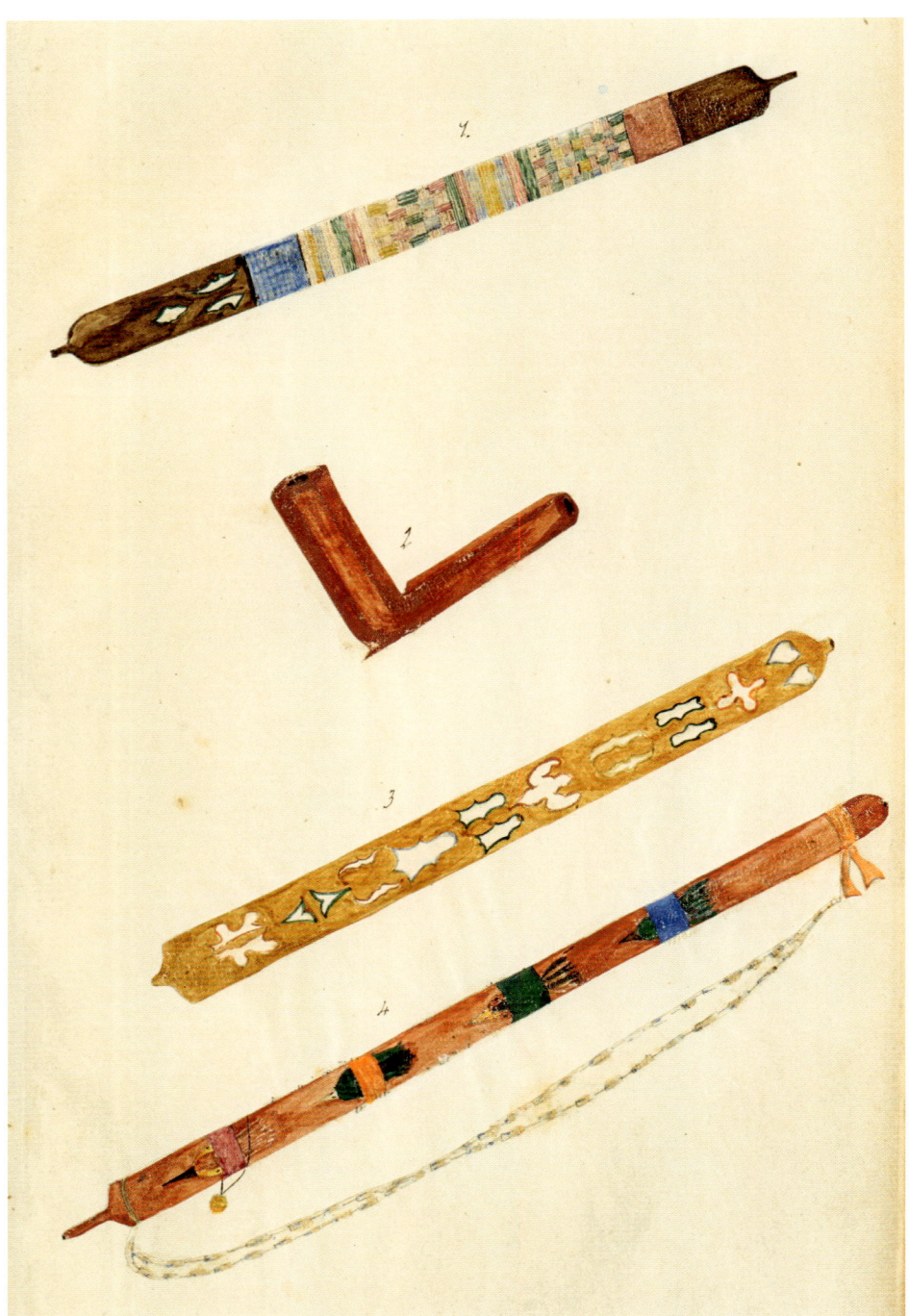

Fig. 52
1, 3, 4 Different Pipe Stems—2 Classic Indian Pipe Head (Calumet).
Drawing by Antoine Marie Gachet ("American Diary," p. 371). Courtesy of the Capuchin Friary,
Fribourg.

In his diary Gachet (1890: 133) recorded the Ojibwa term for catlinite pipe bowls (no. 2) as
"*miskopwokon,* from *opwokon* pipe, and *misk,* red. *Misk* is derived from *miskui, blood*" (cp. Baraga 1853 [1878]: 250–251). No. 4 was identified by Gachet as the pipe of a Chippewa member
of the Wabeno medicine society (catalogue raisonné no. 04) and further described in his account
as decorated with woodpecker skins (Gachet 1890: 178). Calumets were indeed often decorated
with whole skins of the pileated woodpecker (*Dryocopus pileatus*).

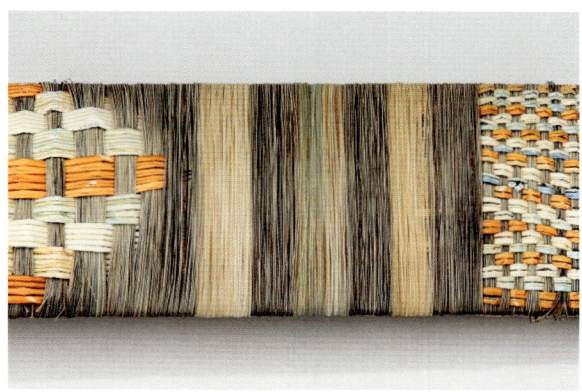

Pipestem

Wood, hot tool marks, horsehair, porcupine quills, silk ribbons, pigments
L 68.8 cm, W 4.8–5.2 cm
Cat.no. 2055 (Catalogue raisonné no. 02)

The exquisite decoration of long-stemmed smoking pipes reflects the importance of smoking in both ceremonial and political contexts. Porcupine quills were traditionally used by the Menominees for this purpose (Skinner 1921: 275, 363), but only a single nineteenth-century example (other than the one collected by Gachet) has been documented (Wisconsin Historical Society, cat.no. 1954.1640, J. S. W. Pardee coll.). Like many other pipestems from the western Great Lakes and eastern Plains region it is wrapped with braided quills to produce geometric and figurative designs (e.g., Flint Institute of Arts 1973: 16–19; King 1977: 51–53).

The present example, which according to Gachet was specifically made for him by a Menominee woman, differs from this style by the use of dyed horsehair wrapped around the stem and partly interwoven with quills in various checkerboard designs (illustrated in Fig. 52 with more elaborate cutout motifs). This style is related to plaited quill-wrapping found on round and flat pipestems from the Great Lakes (e.g., Peabody Museum, Harvard University, cat.no. 94-37-10/51512; Schlossmuseum Gotha, cat.no. 344W). The Menominee use of horsehair in combination with porcupine quills was noted in passing by Skinner (1921: 265).

Three similar examples, at least one of them with horsehair wrapping (King 1977: 39, 53, no. 50; Welsh 1983: 34, fig. 39; National Museum of the American Indian, cat.no. 16/2537, Richard Joste coll.), have been (mis)attributed to the Blackfoot or the Upper Missouri, but are more likely Eastern Sioux work.

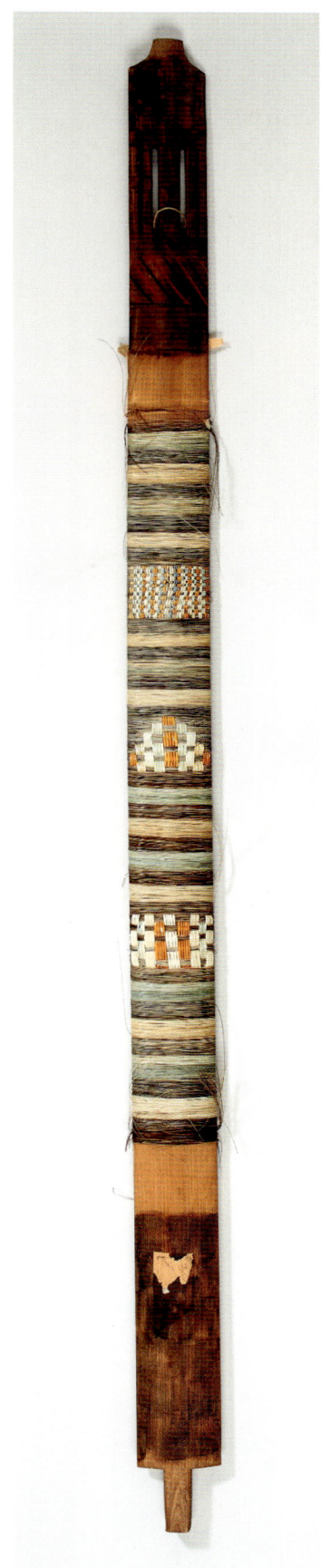

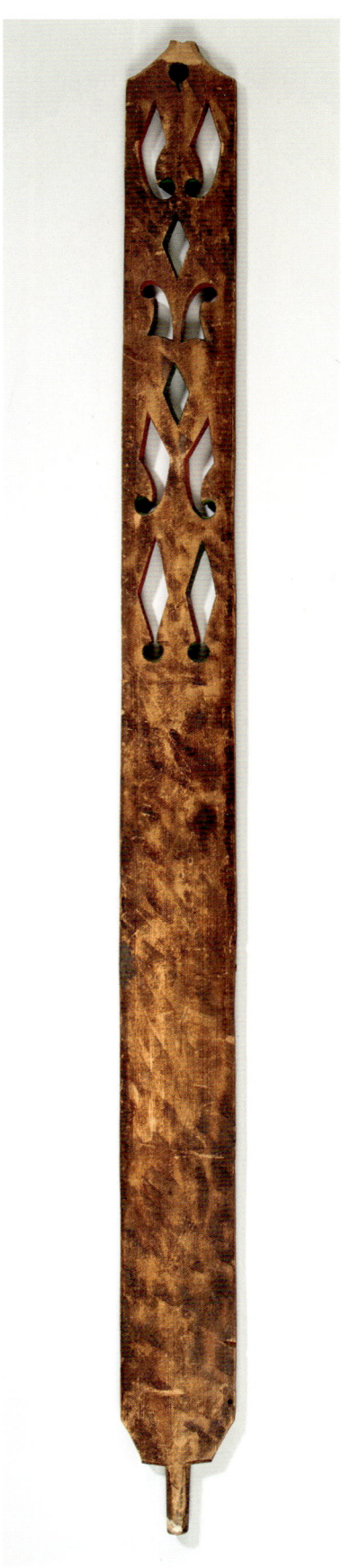

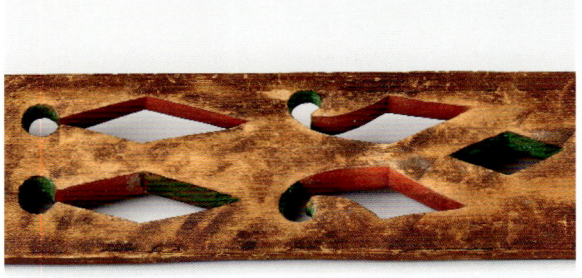

Pipestem
Wood, hot tool marks, pigments
L 90.5 cm, W 7 cm
Cat.no. 2054 (Catalogue raisonné no. 01)

Although lattice or open work in the decoration of flat pieces of wood was widespread in the western Great Lakes region, the Menominees were apparently especially fond of this technique. Stylized floral patterns, diamonds, hearts, chevrons, "war-club" or "lacrosse-stick" motifs (curved with a round end), crosses, and stars executed in this fashion are found not only on pipestems (cp. Fig. 52), but also on cradleboards, heddles, and spoons (see, e.g., p. 72). The appearance of these motifs in engravings on wood and likewise in bead- and quill-work (which in early examples also makes use of negative space) illustrates the fact that they were part of the repertoire of both male and female artisans.

According to Skinner (1921: 133, 268–269, 346), the juxtaposition of red and blue (here seen on the inner edges of the cutout forms) symbolizes for the Menominees the opposition of day and night, summer and winter, or life and death, although blue (or its equivalent green) is not only associated with the west, night, and winter, but also with the south and was regarded as the "holy sky color."

Pipestems of this kind were sometimes referred to as "puzzle" or "trick" stems because the observer was left to wonder how the smoke could pass from the bowl to the mouth in spite of the holes in the wood along the central axis. In order to achieve this "miracle," the maker had to create a bypass around the section of lattice work—no mean technical feat even with the use of metal tools.

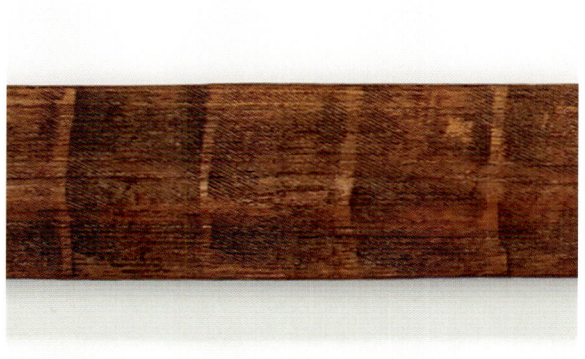

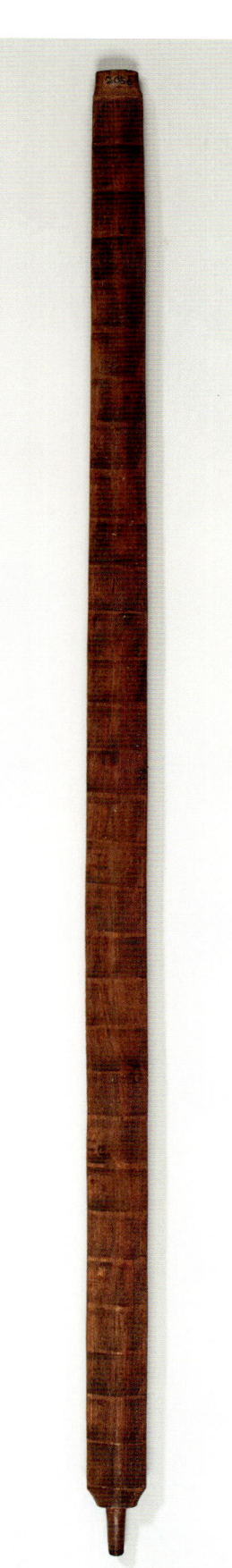

Pipestem
Wood, hot tool marks
L 84.2 cm, W 2.3–3.3 cm
Cat.no. 2056 (Catalogue raisonné no. 03)

Another common method employed by the Menominees and their neighbors to decorate wood was by scorching it with red-hot metal tools such as files ("pyro-engraving"; see also pp. 56, 59, 72).

Other than merely creating a dappled surface texture as in the previous example, the scorching of this pipestem produces a pattern of horizontal bands reminiscent of those found on quill-wrapped stems. A similar pattern is found on a Menominee pipe in the National Museum of the American Indian (cat.no. 19/3074, W. H. Fitzhugh coll.), which in addition features stippling of the scorched bands and some relief carving.

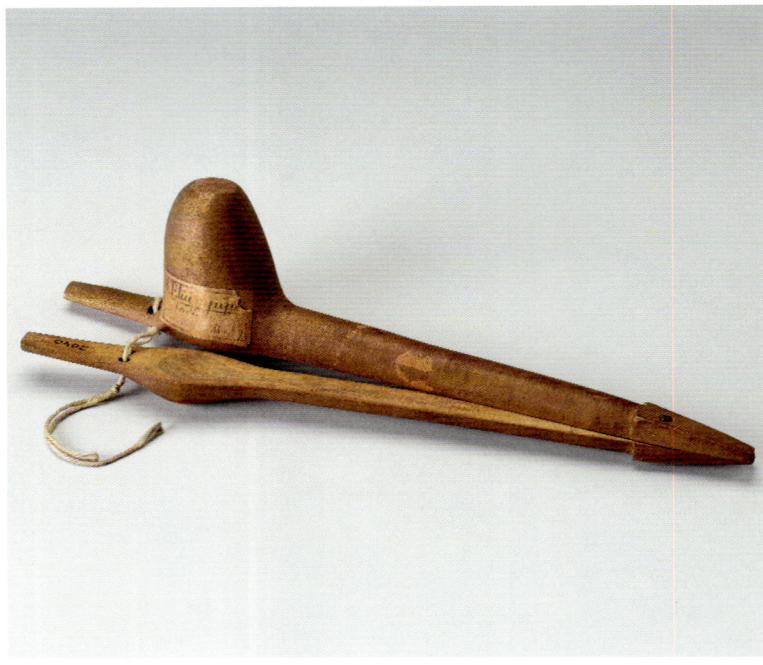

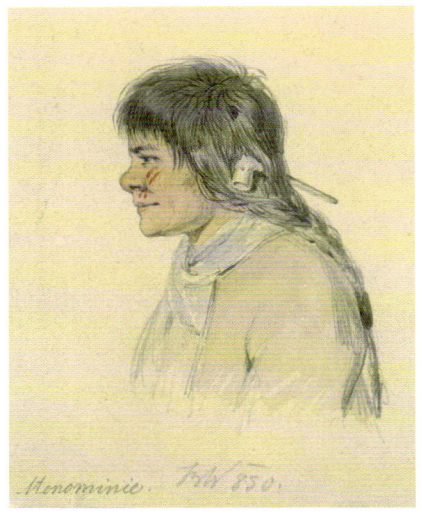

Fig. 53
Johann Baptist Wengler, *Menominie.*
Watercolor, 1850. Copyright Oberöster-
reichisches Landesmuseum, Linz.

Case for clay pipe
Wood, white cotton string, iron nail
L 27.7 cm, H 7.2 cm
Cat.no. 2040 (Catalogue raisonné no. 08)

After the introduction of tobacco in Europe, pipes made of clay, whose form was inspired by models from eastern North America, were commercially produced especially in Gouda in the Netherlands. Already in the seventeenth century these pipes were exported as trade goods to North America, where they began to replace pipes of indigenous manufacture. Special cases of wood or metal, often fitted with a hinged lid at the bowl side and lavishly decorated, were soon made to protect the fragile pipes against breakage (Rapaport 2014).

Because clay tobacco pipes—like many other trade goods—were not "exotic," they were rarely mentioned in ethnographic accounts and hardly ever collected, although for archaeologists they have become an important index for the dating of sites.

The wooden pipe case collected by Gachet among the Menominees appears to be a singular exception. It seems to be of indigenous manufacture and features a pivoted lid unlike those found on European models. A similar closure, with a hinge of wrapped string instead of a nail, is found on needle cases from the western Great Lakes (Cranbrook Institute of Science) and the Plateau (American Museum of Natural History, cat.no. 16/7894).

A drawing by the Austrian artist Johann Baptist Wengler (Fig. 53) illustrates a more common way in which Menominees carried their pipes. In a similar manner one of the men in Samuel Marsden Brookes's painting (see Fig. 15 above) has a clay pipe stuck into his turban, while holding another one in his hand.

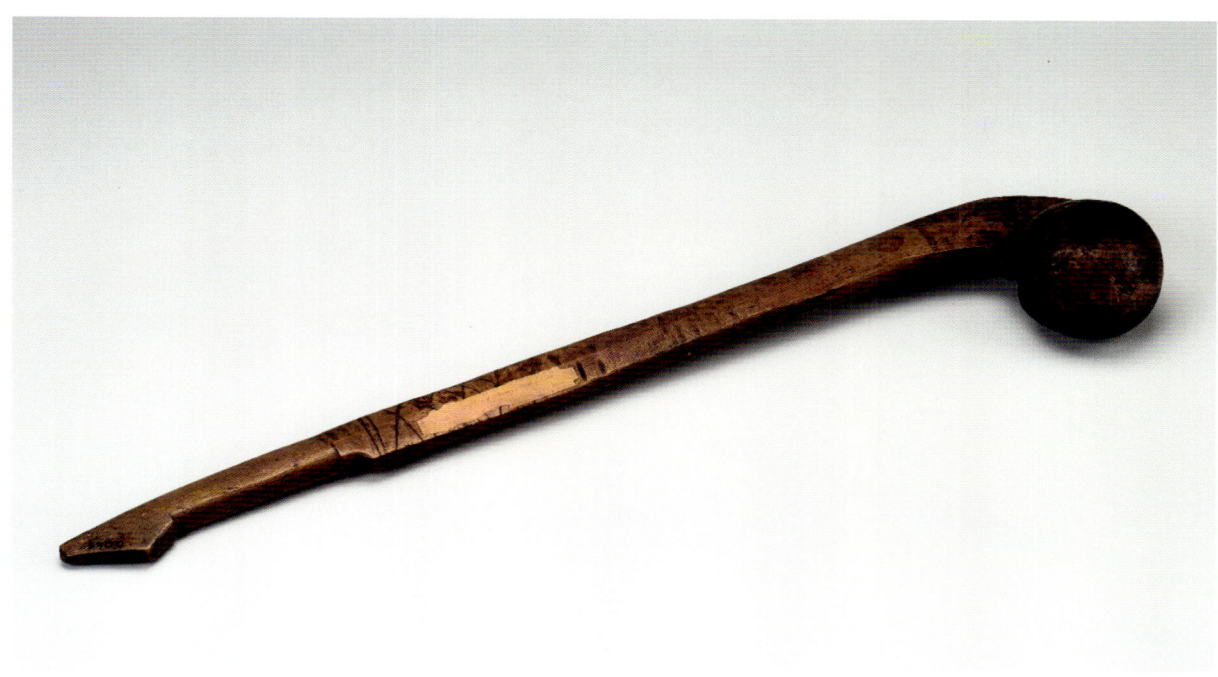

Ball-headed club

Wood, incisions and hot tool marks, traces of pigment
L 52 cm, D (ball) 5.2–6.5 cm
Cat.no. 2041 (Catalogue raisonné no. 09)

Of the two major types of war clubs well attested for the Menominees in the nineteenth century (Skinner 1921: 314–316, pl. LXXXIV; Feder 1964: 36, 54, fig. 19) only the "gunstock club" appears in the contemporary illustrations by King, Catlin, and Castelnau (Kasprycki 1990a: 76, 83–85, 89–90). Gachet (1890: 271) exclusively describes the ball-headed variety ("pakwokosh" or Ojibwa, "paka-makon"; cp. Skinner 1921: 314; Baraga 1853 [1878]: 340) and refers to the presence of such a club in his collection (cp. also Fig. 54). The original label attached to this club is now largely illegible; an earlier typewritten transcription refers to it as "oshko" (probably miscopied from the last two syllables of "pakwokosh") and includes Gachet's explanation of the incised X-marks on the shaft as "indicating the number of enemies killed by the owner."

Ball-headed clubs were widely distributed in north-eastern North America and in the adjoining eastern Plains. The shapes of the documented Menominee examples vary within the general range of the type and exhibit no specific tribal characteristics.

By Gachet's time, clubs were probably no longer used in warfare, but were preserved as heirlooms associated with war deeds of the past and used in ceremonial dances. Miniature clubs of both types were made by those thought to have descended from the Thunderers (the patrons of the warriors) or those who received the club from them in a vision; they were usually tied to war bundles and were supposed to offer supernatural protection and success in battle (Skinner 1921: 316–317). Skinner also notes the frequent painting of clubs in red and black on the opposite sides and associates it with the symbolic opposition of red and blue (see p. 56). The blue paint found on Gachet's club may thus be a substitute for black (Skinner 1921: 317, 346).

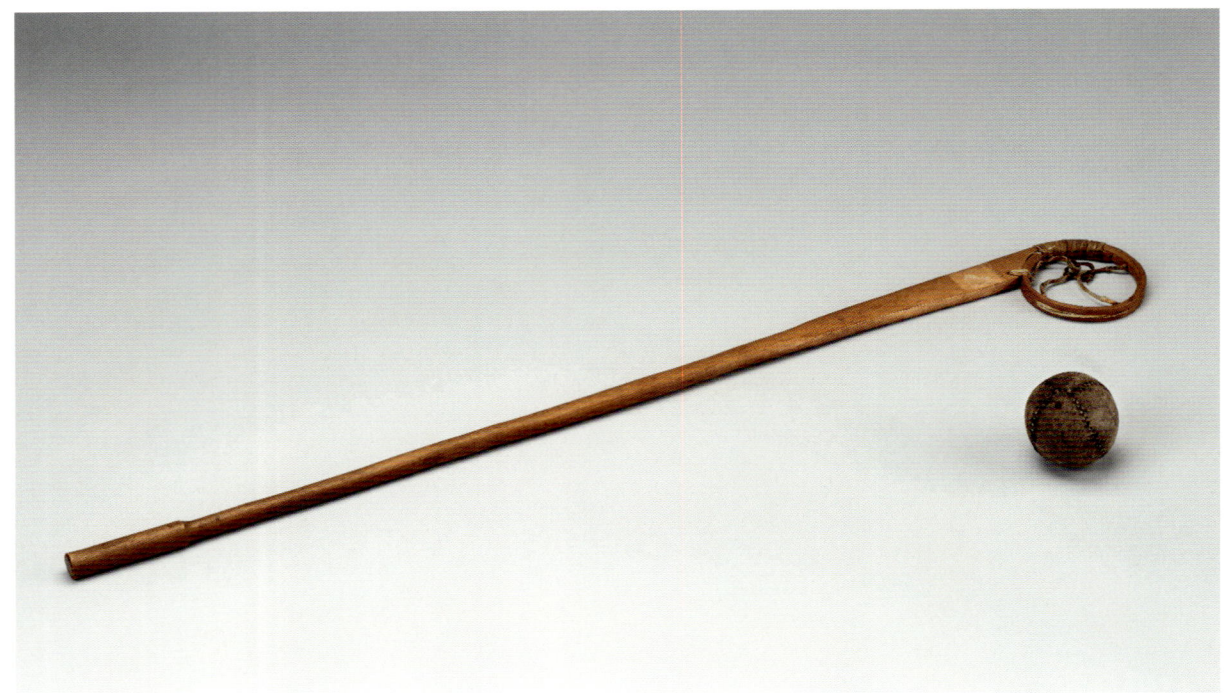

Lacrosse stick and ball

Wood, leather, sinew
L (stick) 65.7 cm, D (ball) 4.8 cm
Cat.nos. 2043, 2039 (Catalogue raisonné no. 10)

Lacrosse (or stickball) is a game traditionally played in most of eastern North America by two competing teams of men attempting to drive a wooden or leather ball with one or (in the Southeast) two rackets over a goal line or at a target. It was generally related to ideas about warfare and was sometimes referred to as the "little brother of war" (Vennum 1994; Culin 1907: 562–616). The term given by Gachet for the stick ("pakath") contains the same root (cp. *pakatham,* 'he strikes it,' Bloomfield 1975: 191) as the term for the ball-headed club ("pakwokosh"), which it also resembles in its outline.

The Menominees considered lacrosse to be the property of the Thunderers, who in the mythical past had played it against the antagonistic powers of the underworld to revenge the death of the culture hero's brother. Often played for the purpose of curing, the game could only be held at the request of someone who had dreamed of the Thunderers or was regarded as the reincarnation of one (Hoffman 1896: 127–136; Skinner 1911; 1913: 55–57; 1921: 56; Densmore 1932: 26–27). That the lacrosse stick collected by Gachet—the oldest documented Menominee example—was made by a Christian Menominee chief may indicate that the game continued to be played for amusement in a secularized form.

Like most other Menominee sticks found in museum collections Gachet's example is of the "pony-foot" variety in which the part of the handle adjoining the ring is broadened and flattened (Skinner 1921: pl. CVI b). The ballstick illustrated by Castelnau (1842: pl. XXXIII, fig. 10; see Fig. 42 above) is probably not Menominee since it was accompanied by a wooden ball not used by them.

Lacrosse reminded Gachet (1890: 273) of "Ballsteck" or "Ballenstecken," a ball game popular in Fribourg in the eighteenth and nineteenth centuries (Staub and Tobler 1881–2017, 10: 1647).

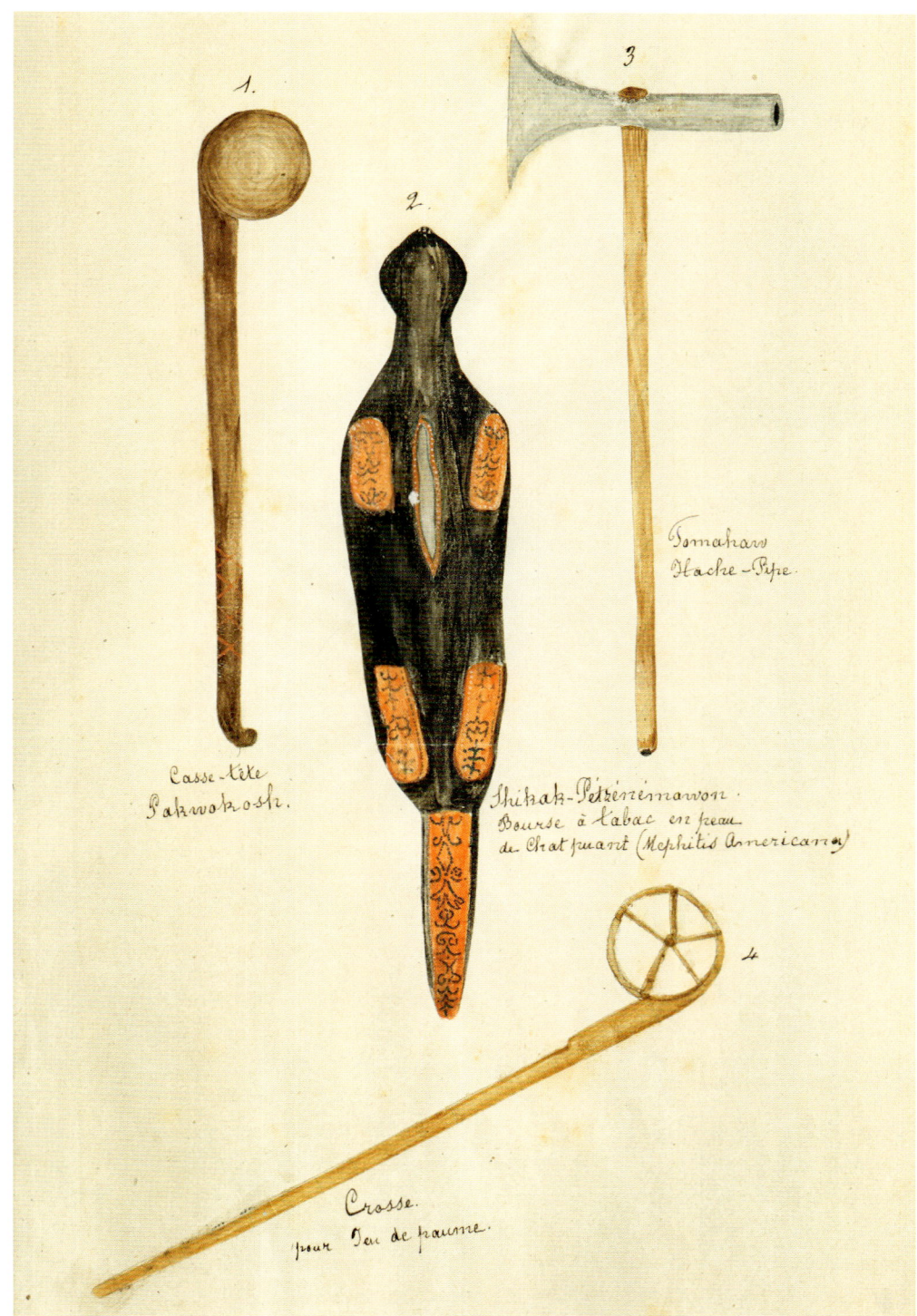

Fig. 54
1 Club—2 Medicine bag of skunk skin—3 Pipe hatchet (Inanapakosheo)—4 Stick for the ballgame.
Drawing by Antoine Marie Gachet ("American Diary," p. 211). Courtesy of the Capuchin Friary, Fribourg.

The pipe tomahawk (no. 3) is not represented in the collection. In his book Gachet (1890: 271–272) refers to the confusion caused by the English use of the term "tomahawk" for the ball-headed club and notes the former use of stone hatchets, whose perforated heads were attached to the handle by means of sinew ("sina") taken from the thigh of a deer (cp. Skinner 1921: 318–319).

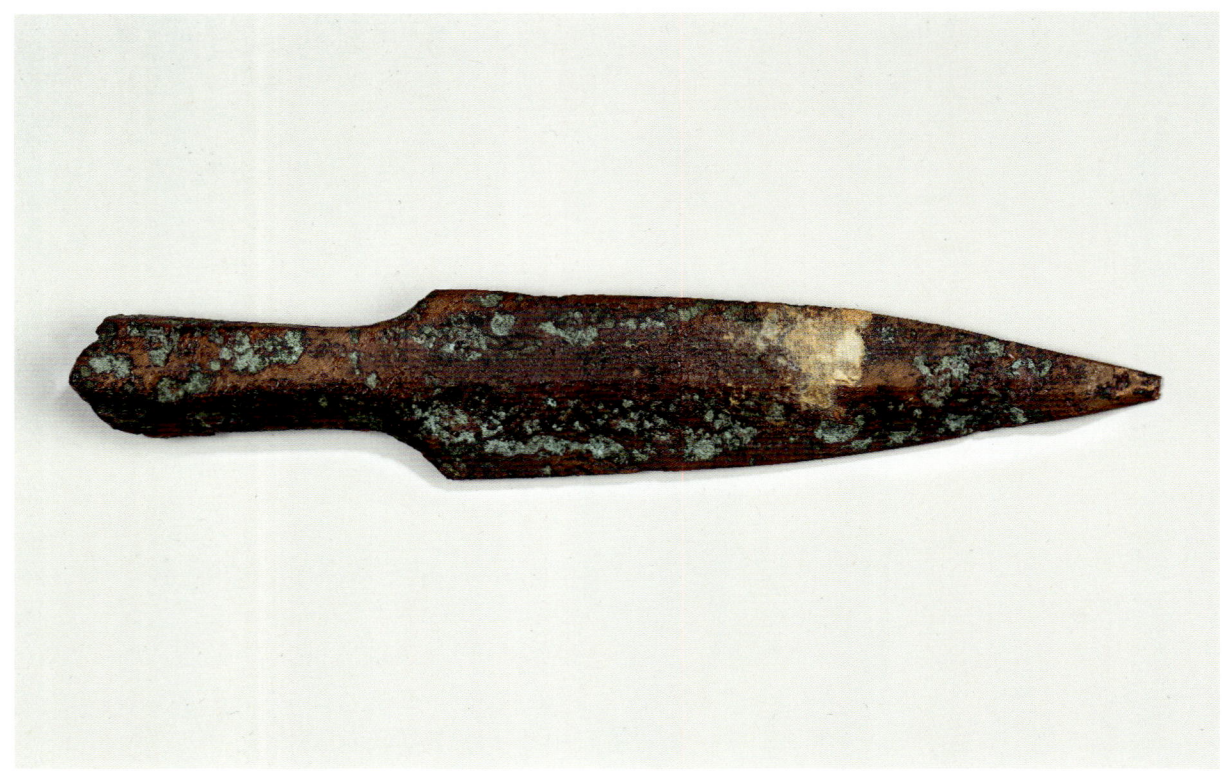

Spearhead
Copper, patined, half socket on base
L 13.6 cm, W 2.3 cm
Cat.no. 2062 (Catalogue raisonné no. 23)

The Old Copper Culture of the western Great Lakes region, dating from 4,000 to 1,000 BC, is the oldest chalcolithic tradition of the world. Surface deposits of nearly pure copper in the area of the Lake Superior permitted the production of spear- and arrowheads, awls, knives, axes, fishhooks, and other tools by means of basically lithic techniques (cold hammering, heating, and annealing) (Griffin 1961). The material was also traded to distant regions, where it was largely restricted to the manufacture of high-status ornaments.

In the nineteenth and twentieth centuries Old Copper artifacts were occasionally picked up as surface finds (Skinner 1921: 280). However, it was only after 1945 that they were excavated from archaeological sites, mostly burial grounds. One of the major sites of the Old Copper Culture in Wisconsin is located in Oconto, about 45 kilometers (30 miles) east of the Menominee Reservation (Ritzenthaler 1979: 8–11).

The procurement and treatment of native copper was still remembered by Menominee elders in the early twentieth century (Skinner 1921: 279–280), although copper from European kettles had replaced it long ago as the material of choice. In Menominee belief, native copper deposits were thought to be guarded by the copper-tailed Great White Bear and the metal was associated with good luck and prosperity (Gachet 1890: 181; Kasprycki 1994: 108).

The point closely resembles in shape and color the one shown on the spear carried by Souligny (see Fig. 25 above), which may well have been a recycled Old Copper artifact.

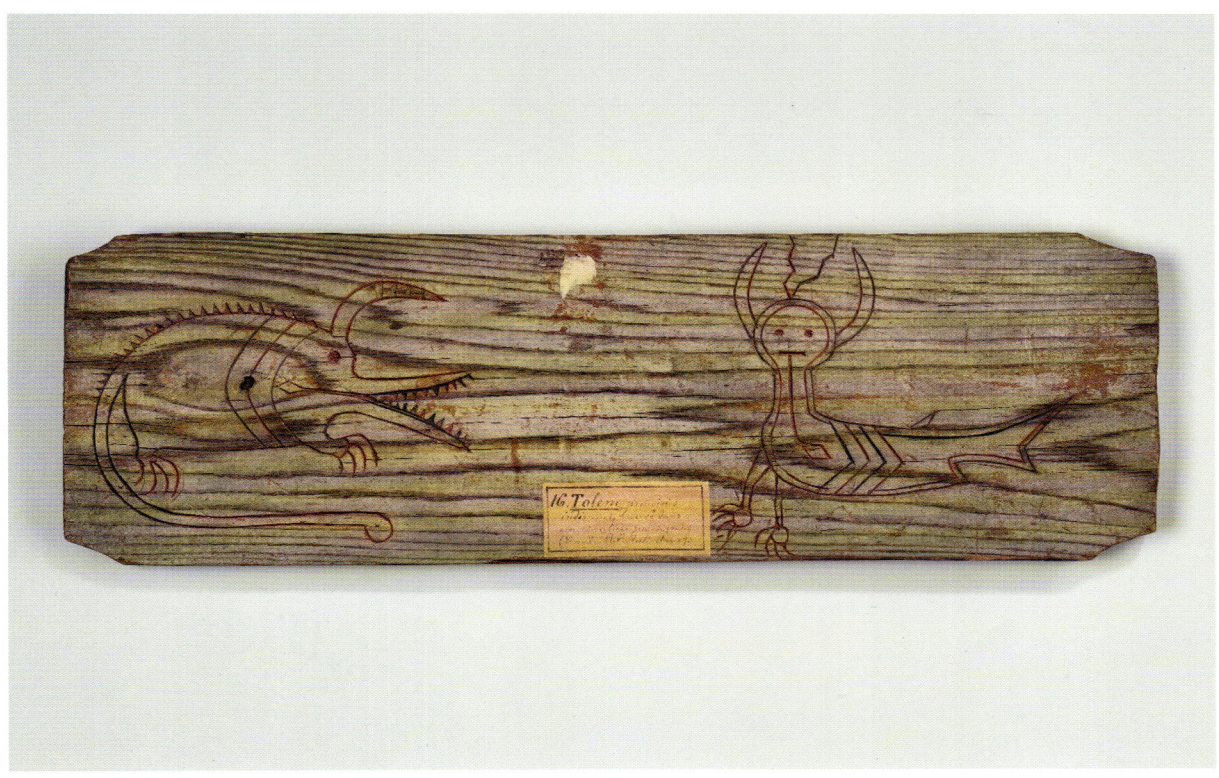

Engraved board
Wood, pigment
L 45 cm, W 13.5 cm
Cat.no. 2036 (Catalogue raisonné no. 16)

Pictographic records on panels of wood or birchbark were made by the Menominees for various purposes. On "song boards" used in connection with the Medicine Society, highly abstracted figures in a linear arrangement served as mnemonic aids for the sequence of complex ritual procedures. On grave markers pictographic signs identified the totemic affiliation and other information relating to the deceased.

The board taken by Gachet in March 1860 from a Menominee grave (see pp. 46–47, Fig. 43), however, is not a grave marker, but—like a comparable board surrendered by a Menominee convert to his predecessor Florimond Bonduel—may best be interpreted as a record of a personal vision, in which the maker had gained access to the support of supernatural beings who are depicted on the board in careful detail.

The figure on the left clearly represents the Great White Bear, the horned and copper-tailed ruler of the underground powers. The image on the right shows a supernatural being with horns, fishtail, and clawed feet that cannot unequivocally be identified with a specific figure from the Menominee pantheon, although it most likely also depicts one of the underworld/underwater powers. Gachet mistakes the bear image for a clan mark of the deceased, and his doubtful interpretation of the second image as a portrayal of the "Sturgeon-Man" also seen on Bonduel's board (and known from Algonquian folklore) was not based on firsthand information. (For a detailed discussion of both boards, see Kasprycki 1994.)

The traces of red and blue/green paint found in the incisions of both boards refer to the cosmic dualism already noted above (p. 56).

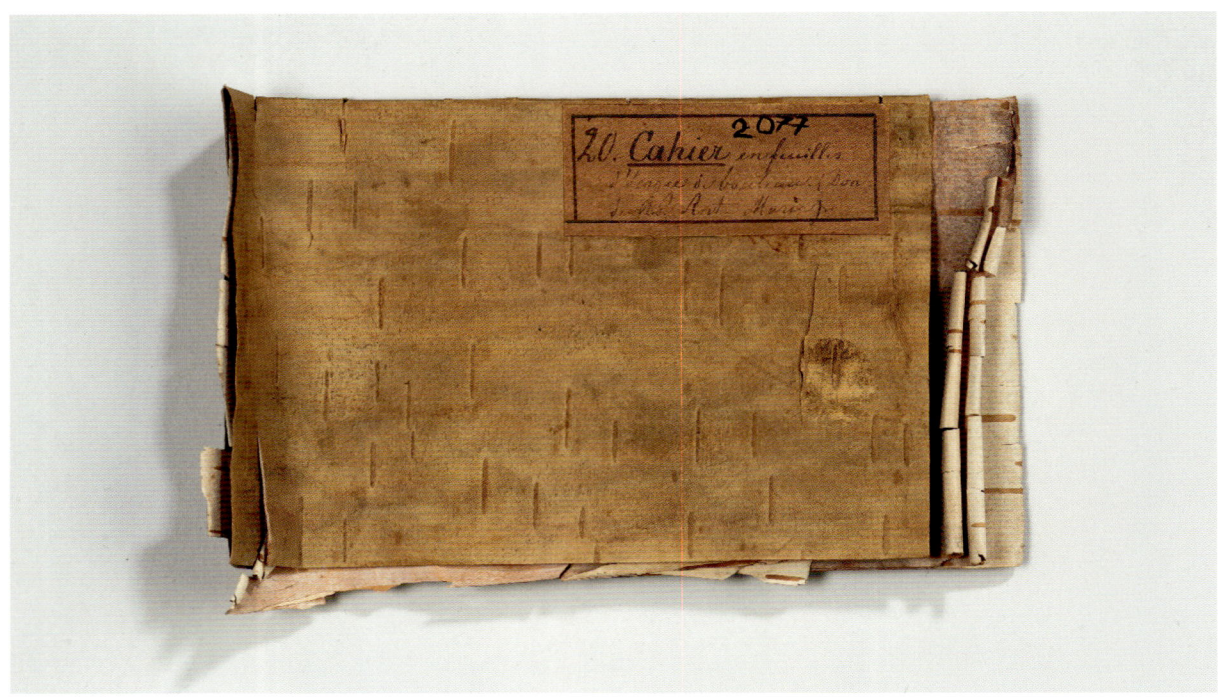

Sheets of birchbark
Birchbark, folded
14.5 × 8.4 cm
Cat.no. 2077 (Catalogue raisonné no. 20)

In addition to its use in the manufacture of canoes and vessels of various kinds and as a cover for wigwams and wrappers for corpses prior to burial, birchbark was employed by the Menominees as a medium for the recording of ceremonial song texts in pictographic writing; in a similar manner representations of supernatural beings and other drawings were incised into the cambium layer of the bark (Hoffman 1896: 107, 239, 254; Skinner 1921: 90–91, 312, 340; Densmore 1932: 70, 90, 102; Kasprycki 2006: 121–122; 2008: 82–83).

Gachet (1890: 225) likened this "papyrus of the North" to parchment or tissue paper and reported that in former times the traders had used it for their accounts and other notes.

In March 1860 Gachet encouraged Okewakew, the daughter of chief Keshena, to write a letter on a leaf of birchbark, signed by "the chiefs and braves of the tribes of the Menomonies," to Pope Pius IX to express the sympathy of the Christian Menominees for his sufferings (Gachet 1890: 230). The Pope's problem had become apparent in 1859 when the new Kingdom of Italy began with the annexation of the Papal States, which despite the protests from Catholics around the world was almost completed by 1861.

The original label identifies the sheets as a "notebook," but there is no evidence for a widespread use of birchbark as a medium for European writing among the Menominees.

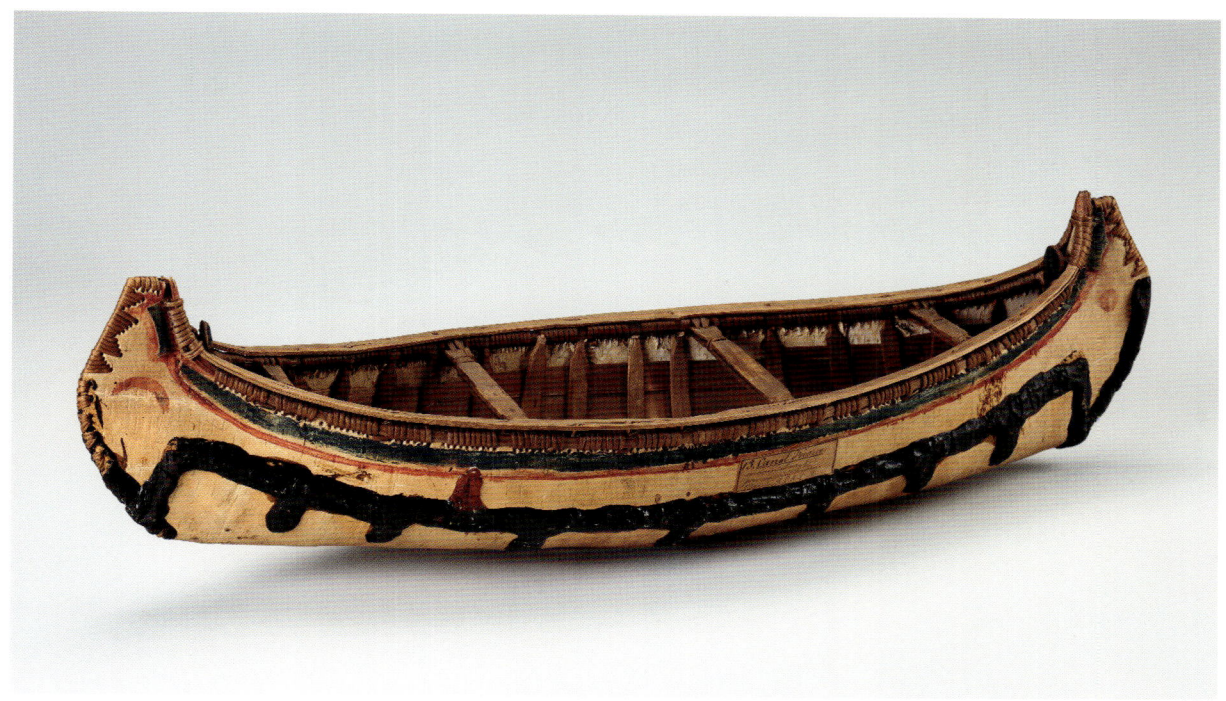

Miniature bark canoe

Birchbark, wood, spruce roots, pigments, resin
L 64.2 cm, W 17.6 cm, H (bow/stern) 16.8–17.7 cm,
(center) 9.3–9.8 cm
Cat.no. 2066 (Catalogue raisonné no. 13)

According to variant traditions, the Menominees were taught the art of making birchbark canoes either by the Great Underwater Panther, by the culture hero Me'napus, or the latter's grandmother (Skinner and Satterlee 1915: 272–273; Skinner 1921: 199–200; Gachet 1890: 196).

The boat was made of sheets of birchbark sewn together with split pine roots and caulked with pine resin by the women, and held in shape by vertical ribs, horizontal lining, a gunwale, and thwarts of cedar carved by the men. Thanks to its lightness the birchbark canoe was the preferred watercraft for long-distance travel involving the crossing of portages (Skinner 1921: 216–222; Gachet 1890: 196, 225–226, 245, 264).

The canoe model presented to Gachet by an old Christian Menominee is a faithful miniature of such boats. Full-sized Menominee birchbark canoes in the American Museum of Natural History (cat.no. 50/9967, A. Skinner coll.) and in the Neville Public Museum show no painted decoration, which is also absent in a drawing by Gachet of a birchbark boat ("American Diary," p. 147). A model in the Denver Museum of Nature and Science (cat.no. 11602), however, features a comparable red and blue design painted below the gunwale. Skinner (1921: 222) was told that men sometimes "painted eyes on the bow and the stern of the canoe so that it 'could see where to go', or added some fancy device."

Birchbark canoes were usually propelled by means of one-bladed paddles. In the nineteenth century, however, both the Menominees and their neighbors also used sails for travel on lakes (see Castelnau's illustration, Fig. 13 above).

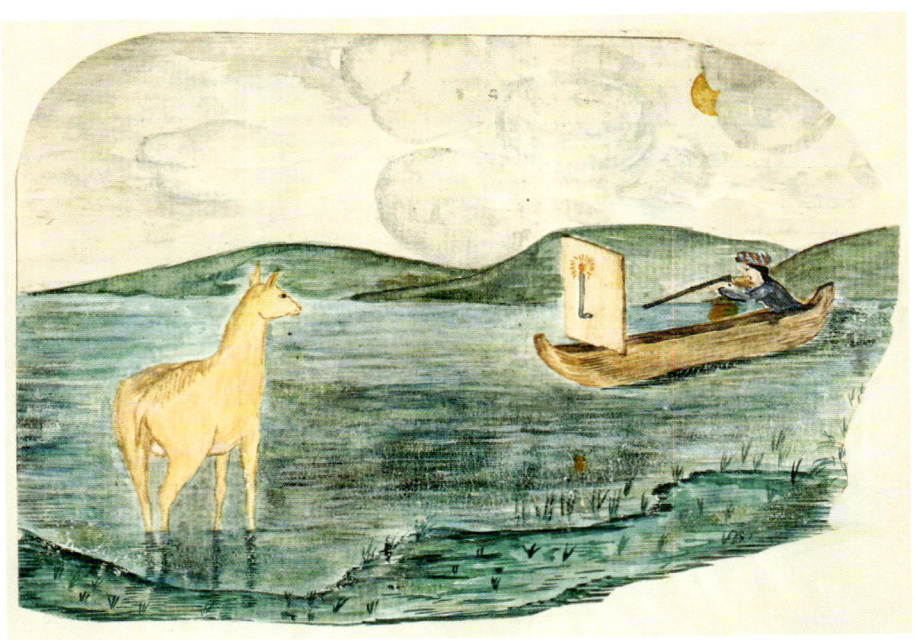

Fig. 55
[Fire Hunting].
Drawing by Antoine Marie Gachet ("American Diary," p. 407). Courtesy of the Capuchin Friary, Fribourg.

Fire hunting is not specifically described by Gachet but is shown in his drawing explaining the use of the jacklight. While firearms had replaced the bow and arrow in the chase, leisters or fishing spears were still employed in fishing. From his cabin on a mound near the banks of the Wolf River Gachet "was often the witness of this torch-fishing; and these lights descending and ascending the water in the midst of a deep darkness offered a spectacle which had a particular charm" (Gachet 1890: 274; cp. also Fig. 47 above).

Miniature dugout canoe with jacklight
Wood, red pigment
L 40 cm, W 8 cm; jacklight: H 17.2 cm, W 3.6 cm
Cat.nos. 2064 (jacklight), 2065 (canoe) (Catalogue raisonné nos. 14, 21)

The dugout canoe was used by the Menominees for travel, hunting, and fishing on lakes and rivers in the vicinity of the villages. It consisted of a log of cedar or basswood, laboriously hollowed out with an adze (Skinner 1921: 222–223, pl. XLVII). Gachet (1890: 146) gives its Menominee designation as "*metikosh*, from *metik*, tree, and *osh*, an ending which signifies all kinds of boats"; cp. *mɛqtekoˑs*, 'dugout canoe', Bloomfield 1975: 119).

The canoe model Gachet had received as a gift from the same donor as the birchbark canoe is fitted with a "jack" (a wooden contrivance for the attachment of a torch, including a reflector) used by both Indians and Whites in the region for nightly fire fishing and hunting (Gachet 1890: 245, 274; Kane 1859: 30–32; Skinner 1921: 185–186, fig. 14). Attracted by the light, fish and game became an easy prey for the skilled hunter and fisher (cp. Figs. 47 and 48). The only documented full-size Menominee jacklights were collected by Alanson Skinner (American Museum of Natural History, cat.no. 50/9837; Canadian Museum of History, cat.no. III-N-24).

No full-size Menominee dugout has been preserved in collections. More than a dozen models in New York, Washington, Chicago, Madison, Milwaukee, and Beloit display some variation of form, including canoes with pointed bow and flat stern, but the shape of Gachet's model is among the more typical ones.

According to Skinner (1921: 360), dugout models were worn by Menominee men as amulets "in accordance with warnings received in dreams, as charms against drowning, and serve to hold tobacco."

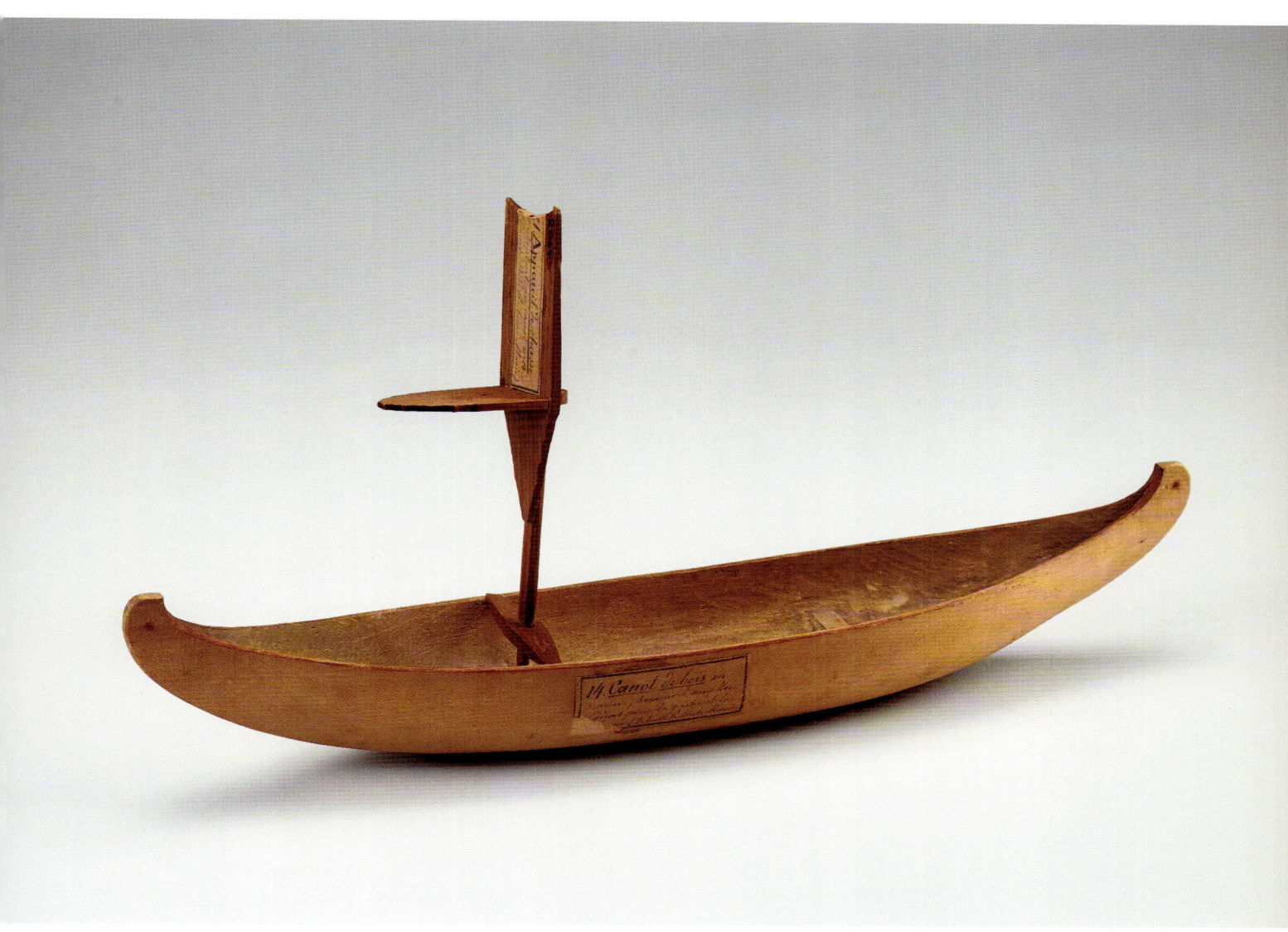

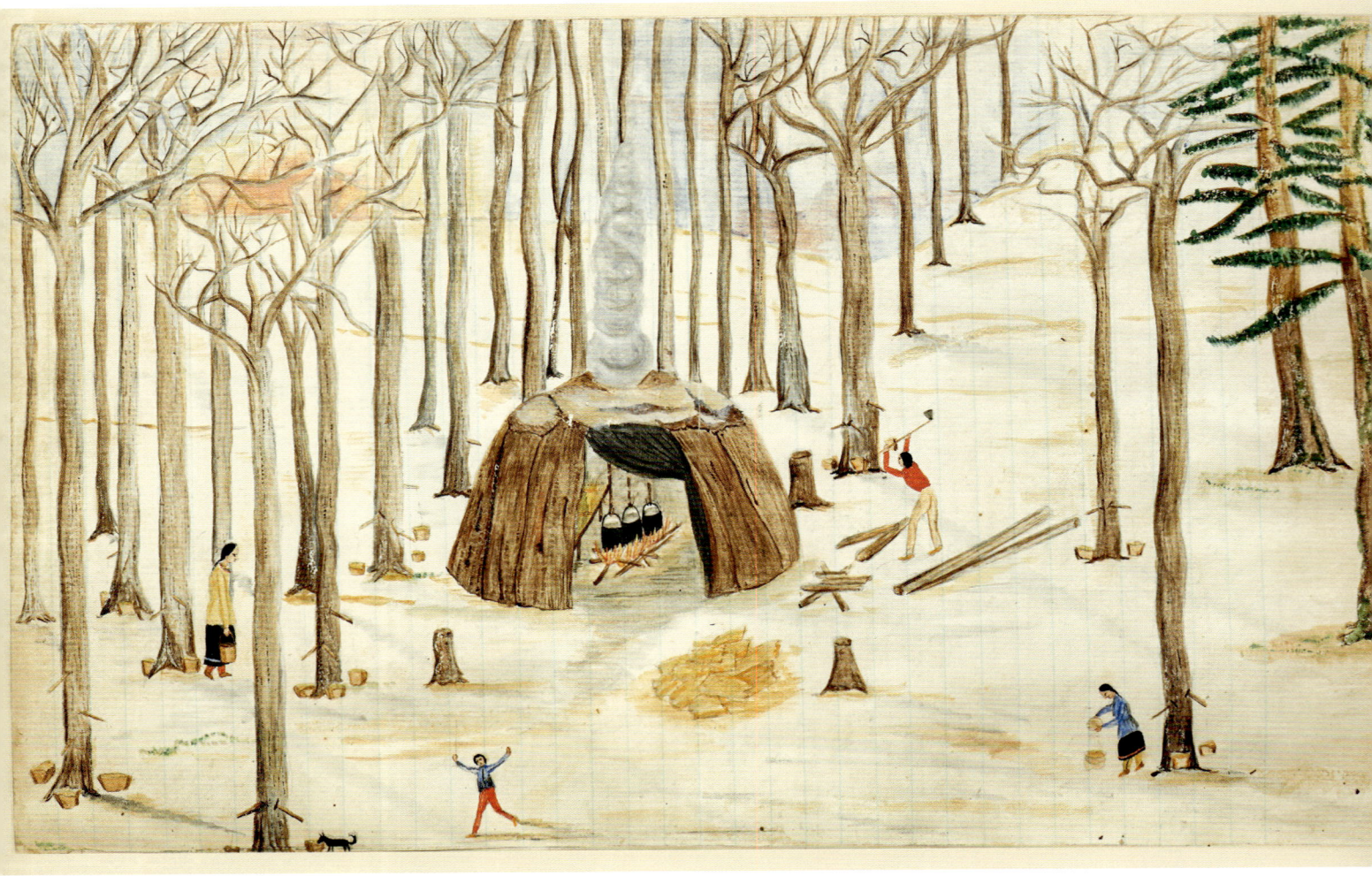

Fig. 56
Maple Sugar Camp.
Drawing by Antoine Marie Gachet ("American Diary," p. 169). Courtesy of the Capuchin Friary, Fribourg.

In March 1860 Gachet visited the sugar camp of a Christian Menominee family in a maple grove across the Wolf River. "The cabin where our host was making his sugar was a log-house, the construction of which reminded me of our Swiss chalets. Cauldrons and pots were hung there, in which the precious maple juice was boiled. Our Indians collect it and bring it in buckets made of birchbark. This juice is allowed to boil until it has acquired a certain thickness and is then poured through a cloth into a barrel to purify it. It is then stirred with a piece of wood until it is reduced to powder. It is in this state that sugar is usually delivered to the market. The more one stirs it, the more the grain becomes fine and white. Our Folles-Avoines have made a name for themselves by the care they put into the preparation of this sugar" (Gachet 1890: 224).

Gachet's drawing shows the kettles suspended over the fire in a traditional wigwam. Trees have been tapped, and the maple sap is dripping from wooden spouts into birchbark dishes. A man is splitting logs for firewood, the women are carrying buckets full of maple sap, and a boy and a dog with a sweet tooth are enjoying the plenty of food after the starving time of the winter months. "It would be surprising in Europe to hear that during a famine, sugar is the only means of subsistence. In a short time the maple sugar makes the Indians overweight, having entered the sugar camp with real Lenten figures" (Gachet 1890: 224).

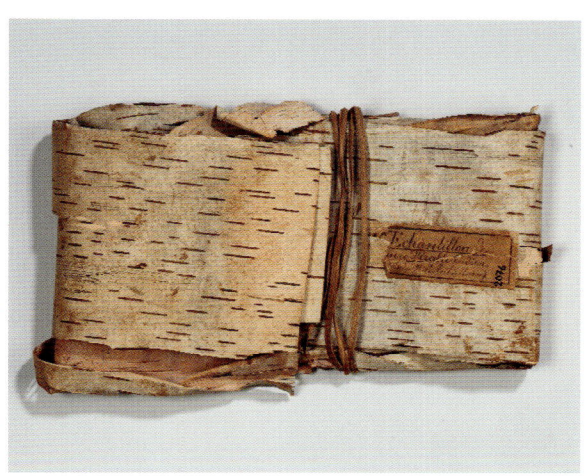
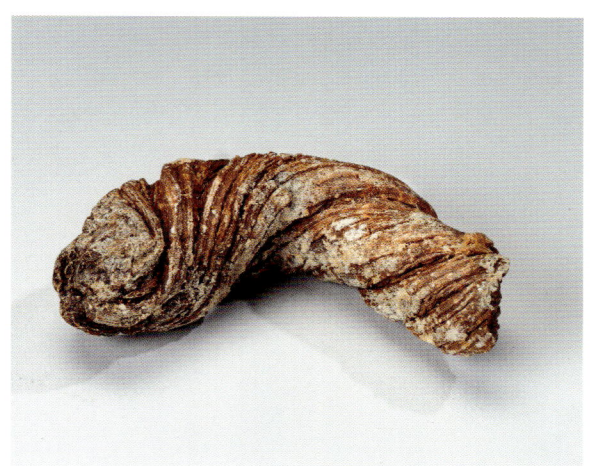

Birchbark wrapper and twisted maple sugar
Birchbark, maple sugar
Wrapper 21.5 × 12 cm (folded), sugar L 15.6 cm
Cat.nos. 2031 (maple sugar), 2076 (birchbark wrapper)
(Catalogue raisonné nos. 15, 19b)

"Our Indians are not content to deliver the sugar to the confectioners. They are themselves confectioners and make candies that our Moosbrugger and Brünnisholz [two confectioners in Fribourg] would be jealous of. Listen to this. They know how to make from maple syrup an appetizing gum that can compete for the delicacy of taste with the most exquisite toffees. The boiling syrup is poured into a bark vase on a layer of snow where it freezes. Sometimes it is eaten in this gummy state, sometimes it is given another form by making what the Canadians call taffy (*de la tire*), making it look like caramel paste of which it has the taste. This is how it is prepared. The Indian takes this gum with both hands, draws it to double length until the gum becomes whitish. It is then twisted, which gives it a rather appetizing appearance. This candy is enclosed in a birchbark envelope and offered as a gift to friends. This envelope is probably far from having the graceful form of a candy box from Paris or Suchard" (Gachet 1890: 225).

In his extensive account of Menominee sugar making, Skinner (1921: 165–172) only briefly mentions the preparation of candy or wax (*se'katkatäo*), which is "pulled, exactly like taffy." Gachet's twisted maple sugar and birchbark wrappers appear to be the only such specimens preserved in collections.

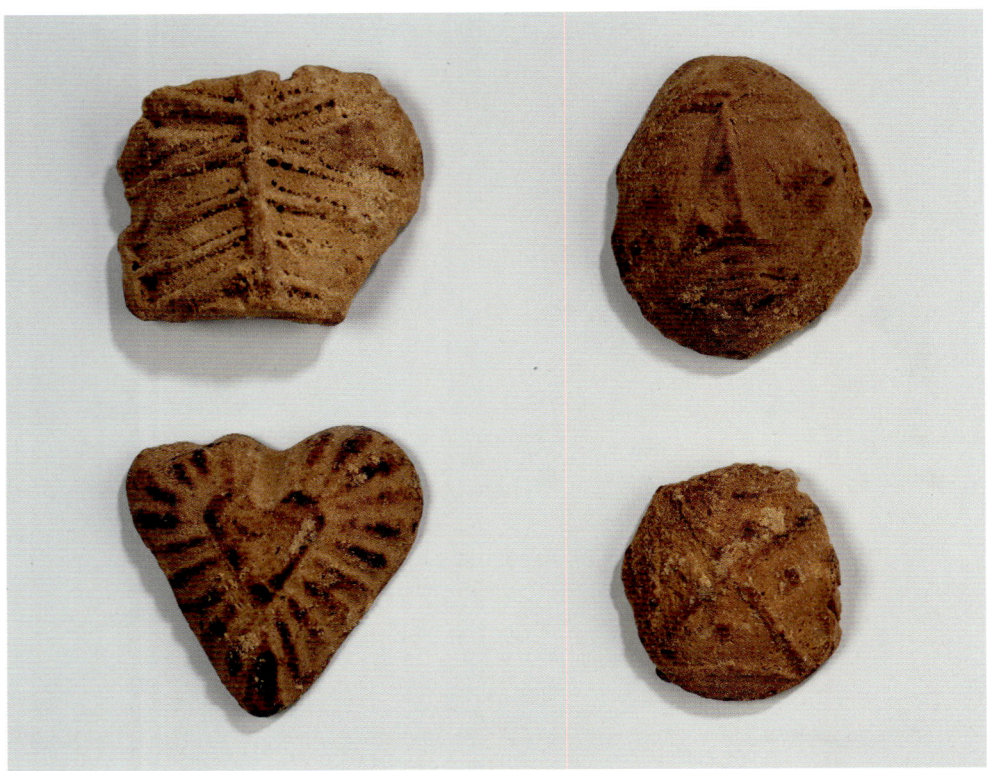

Candies

Maple sugar

Fragment of veined leaf (a) W 7.3 cm; face (b) L 7.1 cm, W 5.8 cm; heart (c) L 7.1 cm; round with cross and four dots (d) D 5.6 cm

Cat.nos. (a, c, d) 2030, (b) 2031 (Catalogue raisonné no. 19a, b)

The Menominees used wooden molds to produce candies in a great variety of shapes (Gachet 1890: 224; Skinner 1921: 170–171). No Menominee mold was collected by Gachet or is found in other museum collections (for Chippewa and Ottawa molds see, e.g., Flint Institute of Arts 1973: 78). Except for the image of a turtle, the samples of candies collected by Alanson Skinner and David T. Vernon (National Museum of the American Indian, cat.nos. 8/2949–2950, 24/2506) show less variety than the fourteen specimens sent by Gachet to Fribourg in two glass jars.

In the absence of any early reports about indigenous maple sugar making, it is today considered a post-contact industry spurred by the European colonists' demand for sugar and facilitated by the availability of metal kettles (Mason 1990). Gachet (1890: 226) was told by some old Indians that in their youth they had still been able to observe sugar making in the old-fashioned way: maple sap had been brought to boil in a wooden trough by means of red-hot stones. It is, however, questionable whether more than syrup could be produced by this method, and the recollections of the old-timers merely appear to indicate a technological development in the production of maple sugar since the eighteenth century.

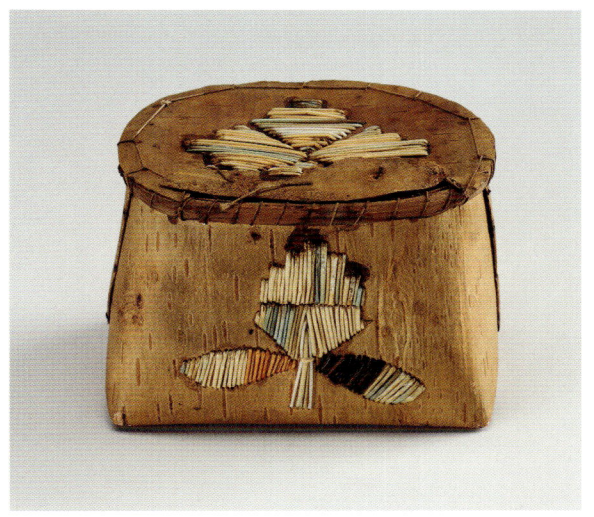
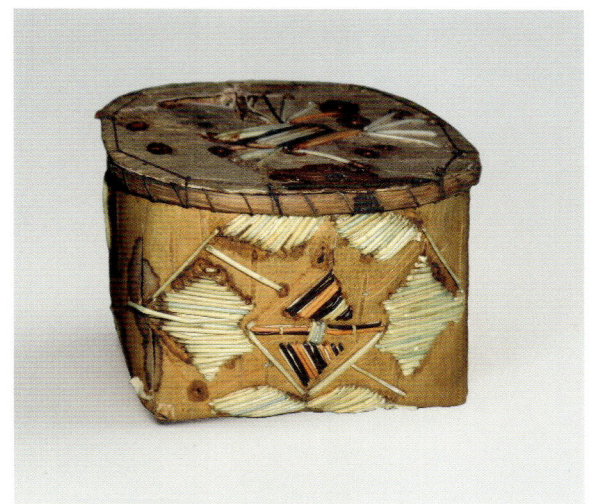

Two mococks containing maple sugar

Birchbark, porcupine quills, yarn
(a) H 6.5 cm, top 8.9 × 5.7 cm, base 9 × 5.2 cm
(b) H 5.8 cm, top 8.5 × 5.9 cm, base 8 × 4.7 cm
Cat.nos. (a) 2010, (b) 2009 (Catalogue raisonné no. 18)

The production and storage of maple sugar was intimately associated with the use of containers folded and sewn from pieces of birchbark with a wood splint reinforcing their rim: especially dishes for collecting the sap, buckets for transporting it to the sugar camp, and boxes to keep the sugar for later consumption (Skinner 1921: 165–168, 294–294). Many of these objects could be quickly made and were rarely decorated, although some boxes featured flat, light-colored designs scraped from the dark outer layer of the winter bark (e.g., American Museum of Natural History, cat.no. 50/4828, W. Jones coll.; Newark Museum, cat.no. 42.22, A. Skinner coll.).

"Mocock" is an English loan word derived from Ojibwa *makak*, 'box', to designate all kinds of birchbark containers. Gachet (1890: 225) gives the Menominee designation as "Mokaw" (*maka·h*, Bloomfield 1975: 107).

With the adoption of the technique of quillwork on bark (see p. 75), in which dyed and unflattened porcupine quills were inserted at both ends into holes pierced into birchbark by means of an awl, and the growing market for maple sugar in American cities at a price far below that of cane sugar, quilled sugar boxes became a popular industry among the Menominees and their neighbors. An oval lid of bark, also quilled, was sewn to the top of these mococks to avoid spilling their sweet contents during transportation (cp. also Fig. 42, no. 7).

"Nothing is cuter," Gachet (1890: 261) wrote, "than the little maple sugar boxes made as gifts that they cover with embroidery of this kind. The reader must not be surprised that the art of embroidery has thus penetrated the forests of the New World." Remarkably few Menominee mococks have been preserved in museum collections.

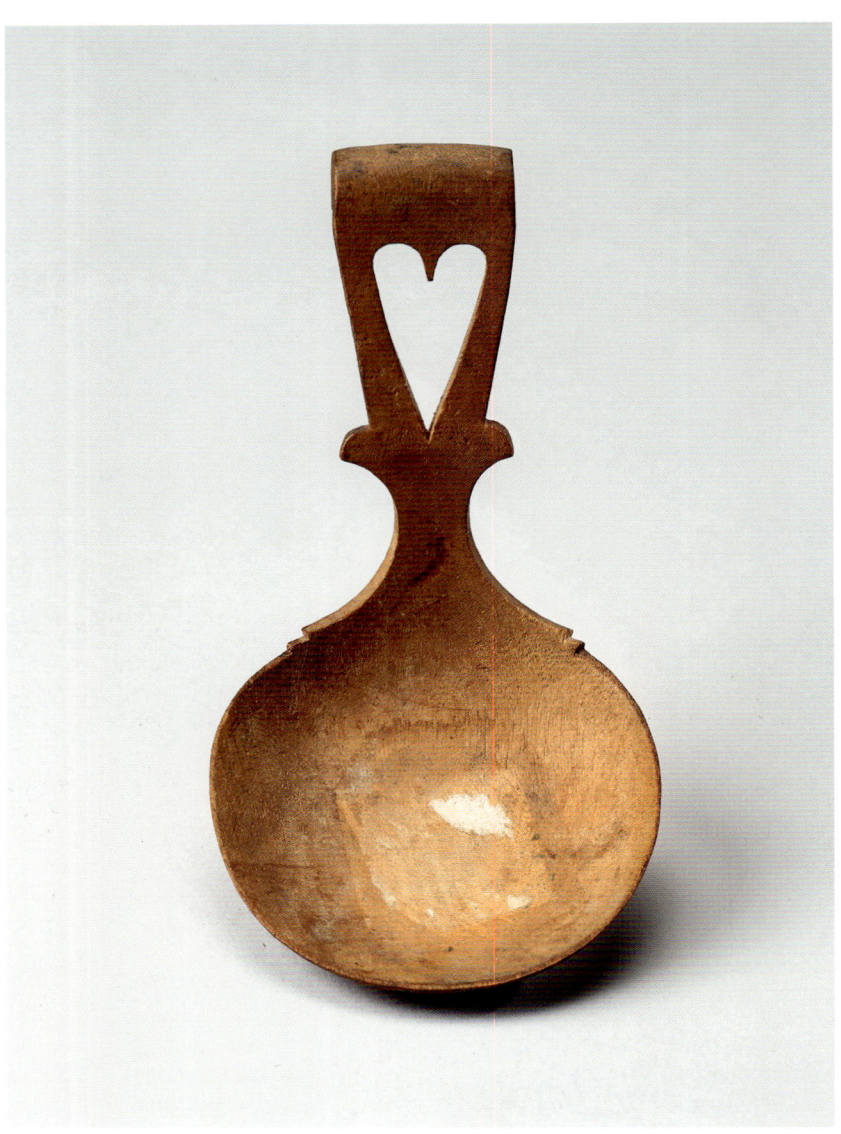

Spoon
Wood, hot tool marks on the edges of the handle
L 11.8 cm, W (bowl) 6.2 cm
Cat.no. 2037 (Catalogue raisonné no. 22)

In his written account Gachet (1890: 272) only briefly refers to wooden spoons by the Ojibwa term "emik-won" (*emikwân*, Baraga 1853 [1878]: 112; cp. Menominee *ε·meskwan*, Bloomfield 1975: 46) in connection with the carving of bowls from maple wood, which "they know how to give the most pretty polish." The spoon found in his collection is an especially nicely carved example with a delicate outline and an open-

work heart on the handle. It shows no signs of wear or patina and may have been a gift to the missionary or made for him on commission.

More than half a century later Skinner (1921: 289–292) found the maple, birch, red cedar, and walnut spoons of the Menominees to be "not so well made as those of their neighbors." Effigies carved at the end of the handle are rarely found on the specimens preserved in museum collections in Milwaukee, Madison, Chicago, New York, and Washington, and openwork mainly consists of simple geometric forms.

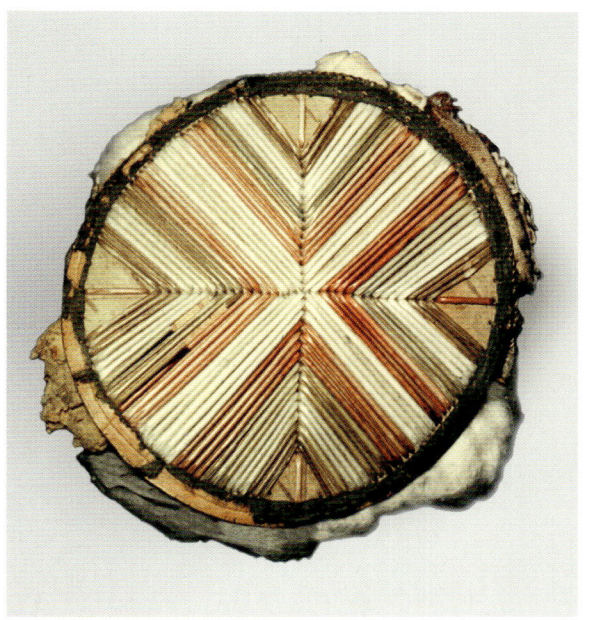 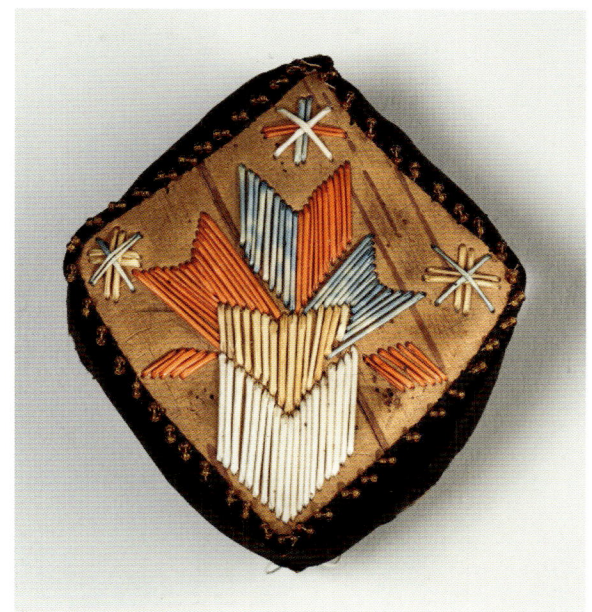

Two pincushions
Round: birchbark, porcupine quills, silk ribbon, woolen fabric; leather, cotton fabric, and unbleached cotton filling; cotton yarn
D 9 cm
Diamond-shaped: birchbark, porcupine quills, glass beads, cloth; cotton filling; cotton yarn
L 8.2 cm, W 7.4 cm, H 2.5–3.4 cm
Cat.nos. 2013 (round), 2014 (diamond-shaped) (Catalogue raisonné no. 17)

Just as new forms of knifesheaths emerged in North America as a result of the introduction of steel knives, traditional containers for bone needles (such as bone tubes) were replaced by new kinds of artifacts used to store and carry steel needles, which had revolutionized indigenous sewing practices since the sixteenth century.

In the western Great Lakes region needlebooks and pincushions were in the nineteenth century often made of birchbark decorated with porcupine quills and produced both for the use by Native women and for sale. For missionary collectors these nicely made parts of a sewing kit illustrated the industry as well as the taste of their makers on their pathway to "civilization."

In addition to the forms collected by Gachet, heart-shaped or pouch-like pincushions were common and are documented for the Ottawas of Michigan (Graham 1983: 28, 50). Decorative panels of Menominee needlebooks are in the Logan Museum of Anthropology (cat.no. 6933ab, Glen Ridenour coll.). Similar panels for a pincushion in the Neville Public Museum (cat.no. 11.212) are undocumented, but may well be Menominee.

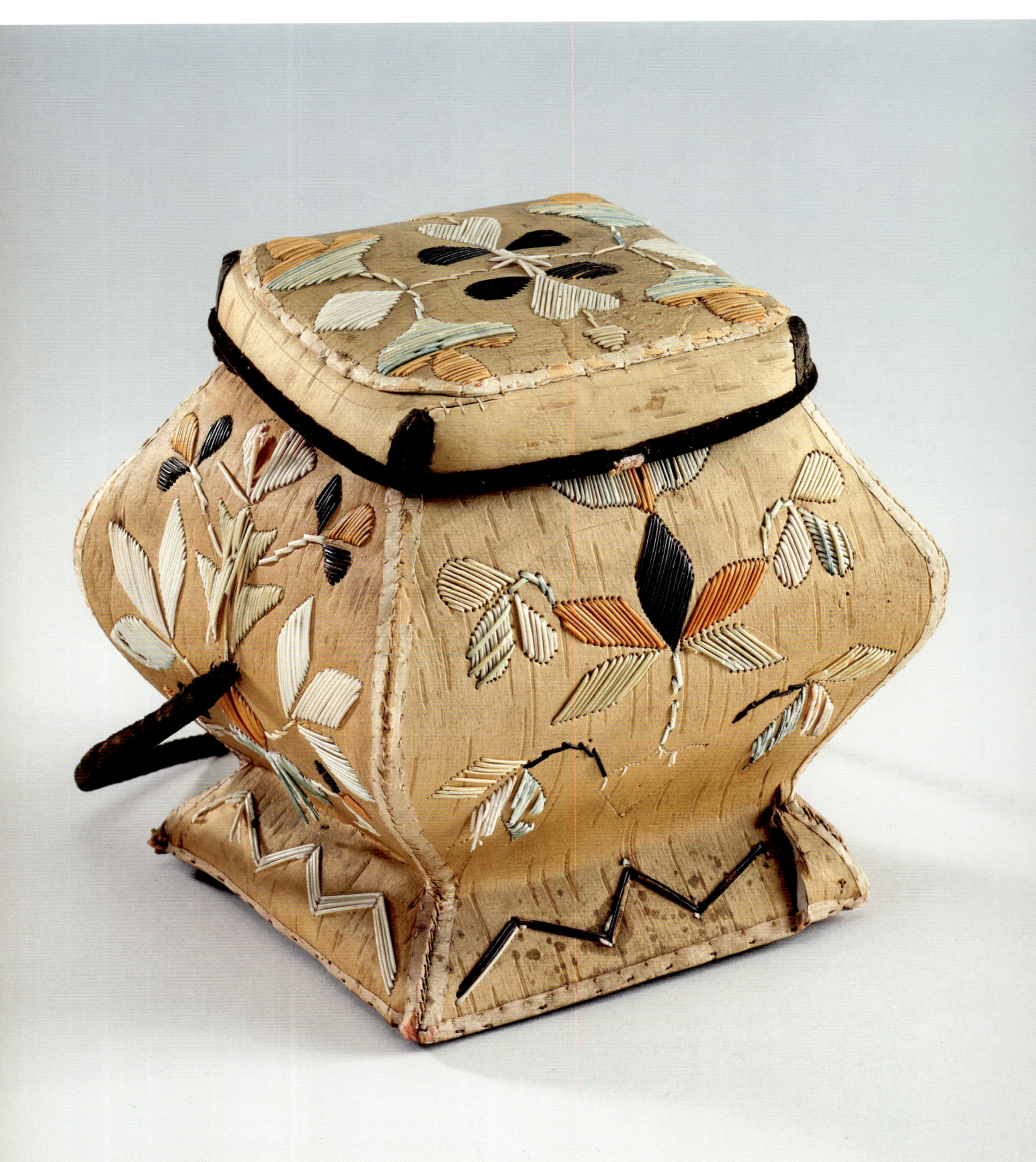

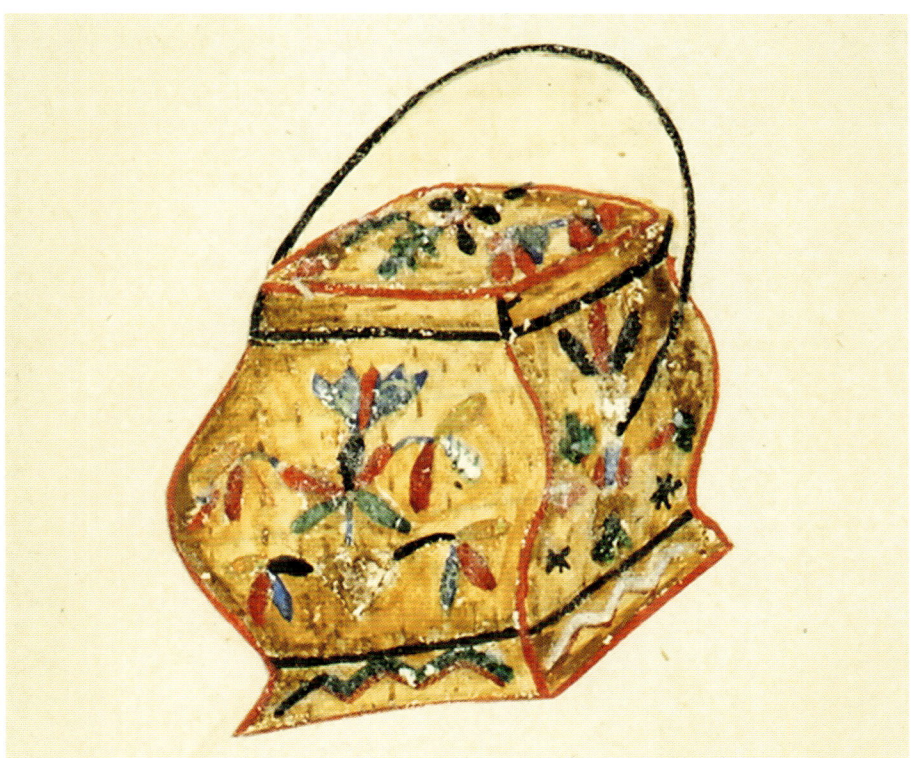

Fig. 57
Sugar Box.
Drawing by Antoine Marie Gachet ("American Diary," p. 383. Courtesy of the Capuchin Friary, Fribourg.

Gachet's drawing of a quilled birchbark box clearly resembling the one in his collection illustrates the limits of his artistic capabilities but conveys an accurate sense of the prevalent style.

Lidded birchbark box
Birchbark, porcupine quills, velvet, silk ribbons, paper
16.5 × 12.5 × 16.7 cm, base 13.5 × 14.5 cm
Cat.no. 2008 (Catalogue raisonné no. 12)

The decoration of birchbark objects with dyed porcupine quills first emerged among the Mi'kmaqs in Nova Scotia and New Brunswick probably in the early eighteenth century (Whitehead 1982) and by the time of the American Revolution had spread to the eastern Great Lakes. It was apparently only after 1815 that it suddenly and vigorously appeared in the western Great Lakes region, where—like in the Canadian Maritimes—it was used on a broad range of indigenous goods produced for the Euro-American market and in this context also served as a marker of indigenous identity (Phillips 1998).

The earliest known specimens of this kind made by Menominee women date from around 1830 and show an already fully developed canon of shapes (including traditional mococks [see p. 71] as well as bowls and boxes with pedestals reflecting the tastes of the market) and of designs (in which the abstract, floral, and pictorial designs of quillwork on leather were further developed and adapted to the possibilities of the new technique) (Kasprycki 2007: 116–117). Both shapes and designs were largely shared with the Ottawas of Michigan (e.g., Graham 1983: 29, 34; Kasprycki 2008: 73).

By 1860 a number of changes had taken place, notably the replacement of seams and edgings of root splints by silk ribbons or velvet, a simplification of the floral, and a disappearance of the pictorial motifs. It seems that the Menominee production of quilled bark objects lagged far behind that of the Ottawas and Chippewas.

Pieces of a January 1860 newspaper lining the inside of the box indicate that it was made immediately before being shipped to Fribourg.

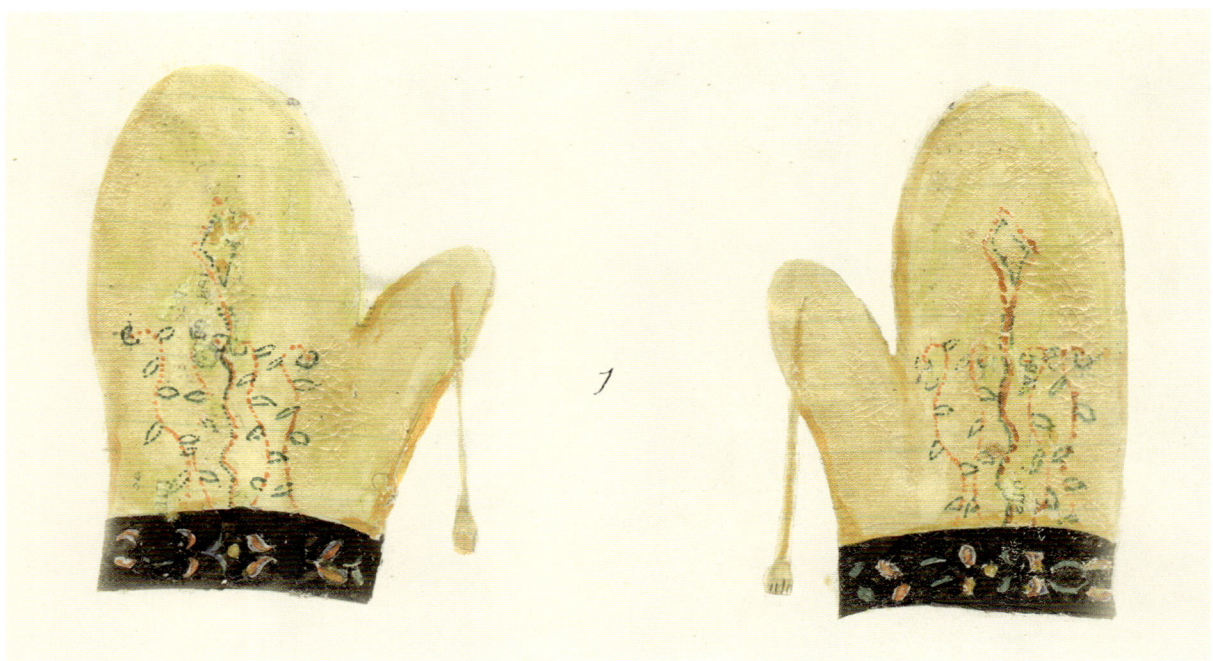

Fig. 58
Mittens.
Drawing by Antoine Marie Gachet ("American Diary," p. 335). Courtesy of the Capuchin Friary, Fribourg.

The style of decoration (most probably done in beadwork) on the cloth-backed cuffs of this pair of mittens more closely resembles the one found on the moccasins illustrated in another drawing (Fig. 59) than the mittens actually collected by Gachet. The pattern on the leather part of these mittens is also known from examples of Menominee quillwork.

Mittens

Buckskin, glass beads, silk ribbon, cotton yarn
L 25.5 cm, W 12.5 cm
Cat.no. 2001 (Catalogue raisonné no. 29)

In Wisconsin and other parts of North America where winters are usually very cold, mittens were part of the dress of indigenous peoples (gloves were an introduction from Europe). For White collectors, however, they did not have the same attraction as, e.g., moccasins, and this pair is apparently the only Menominee example to have survived in museum collections. Skinner (1921: 221) noted their manufacture by the Menominees, but did not include them in his vast collection now scattered in many American museums.

Although mittens are pre-European, the majority of the few examples known from other parts of the North American Subarctic and Woodlands regions were either made by the Wendat (Hurons) for the tourist trade (decorated with moosehair appliqué) or by the Canadian Métis (decorated with mostly floral quillwork).

Openwork bead appliqué, in which the centers of the design elements remain blank, is a style often found on earlier Menominee works in line quillwork and its derivatives (see p. 80). The specimen collected by Gachet shows no sign of wear and may have been made as a gift or for sale.

In one of his drawings (Fig. 58) Gachet illustrates another pair of broadly similar mittens whose cuffs are edged with cloth and with tassels dangling from the thumbs. The tassels seem highly impractical for outdoor work in winter and may indicate that this pair was made for children.

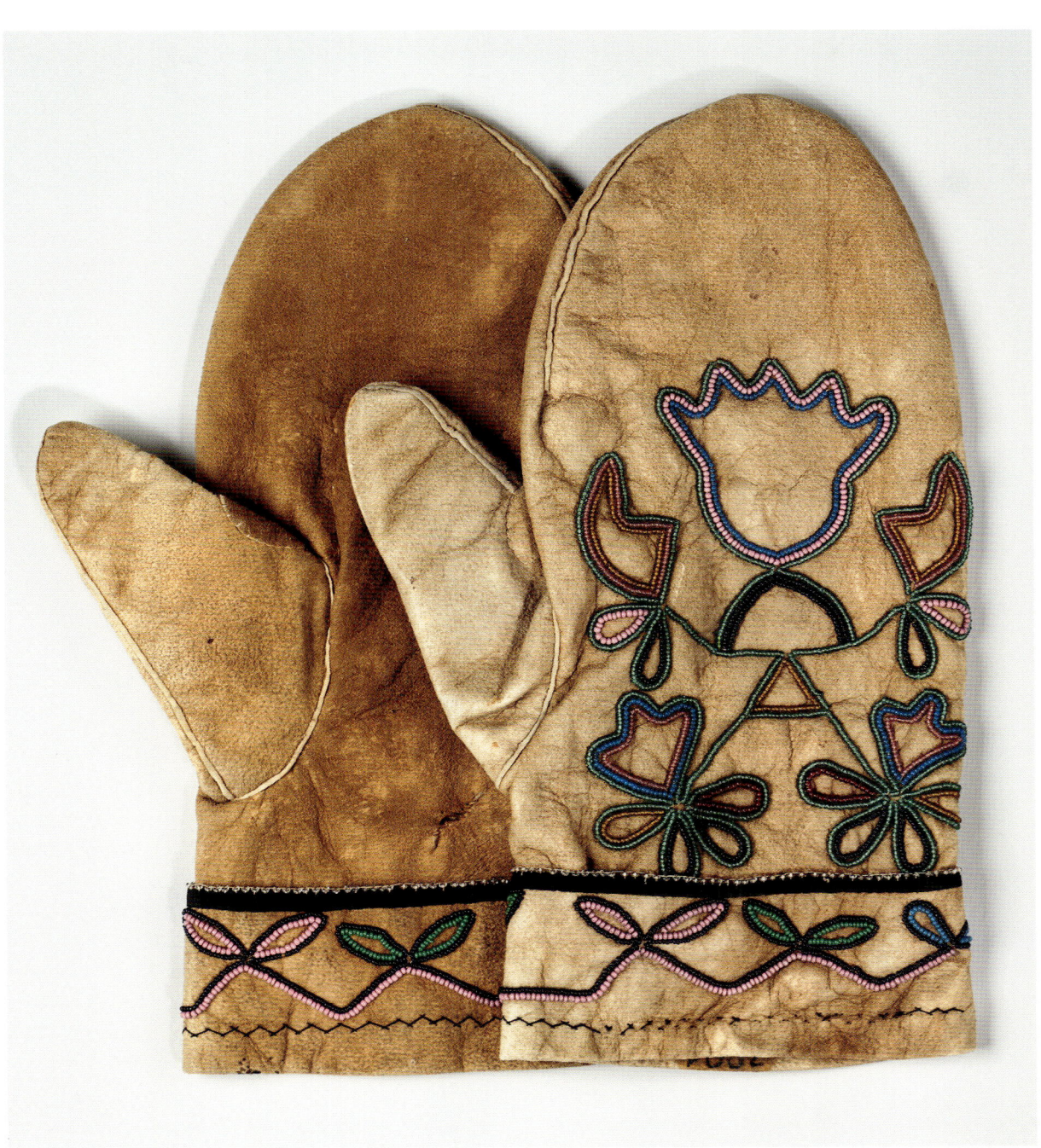

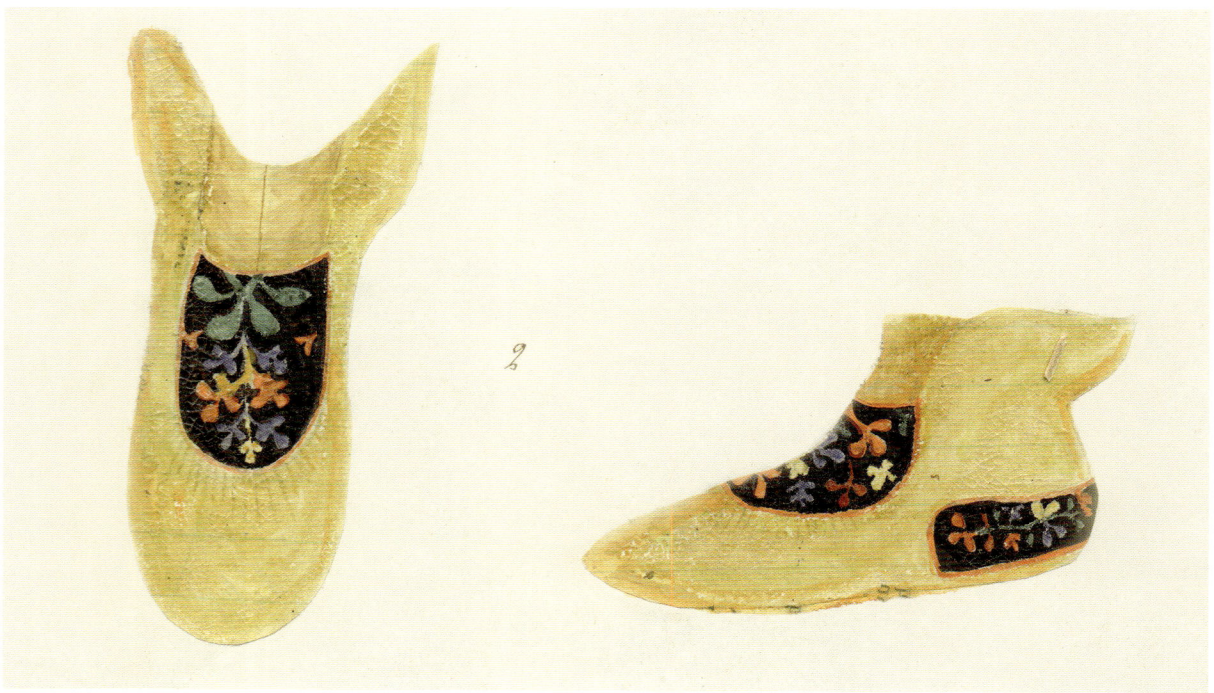

Fig. 59
Moccasins.
Drawing by Antoine Marie Gachet ("American Diary," p. 335). Courtesy of the Capuchin Friary, Fribourg.

"This foot covering is what every Indian wears, men, women, and children. They are made of the skin of the stag or the fallow deer, which the Indians know how to tan with the brains of the same animal. The front part is covered with a piece of skin of a richer color upon which the women embroider, with beads or porcupine quills in diverse colors, figures in the Indian style. Another piece, embroidered in the same manner, covers the sides of the feet above the heel" (Gachet 1890: 153).

Moccasins
Buckskin, cloth, silk thread, glass beads, silk ribbons, cotton fabric, cotton yarn
L 25.5 cm, W 10 cm, H 9.5 cm
Cat.no. 2005 (Catalogue raisonné no. [30])

Although this pair of moccasins is merely listed as coming from North America in the 1940 inventory, it can be safely attributed to the Menominees and almost certainly to the Gachet collection.

In the early nineteenth century Menominee moccasins were made of a piece of buckskin with a T-shaped heel seam and the front part of the leather turned up and sewn with a puckered seam to a semi-oval apron decorated with porcupine quill appliqué. Another piece of buckskin was sewn to the rear part and folded over as ankle flaps often decorated in the same manner (see, e.g., Penney 1992: 73–74, no. 4; Kasprycki 2007: 118, fig. 9). The delicate quill decoration, executed in linework, consisted of highly stylized and symmetrical floral patterns in openwork without a filled-in background, which are also found on medicine bags and knife cases. (No known examples have been preserved of an earlier cut, suggested by Skinner [1921: 117], with both straight heel and toe seams.)

By the 1860s quillwork had largely given way to appliqué beadwork, the floral patterns tended to become more realistic and often less symmetrical and were sometimes sewn on dark cloth. A pair of this style was drawn by Gachet to illustrate the manuscript of his "Five Years in America" (Fig. 59).

The pair in the Fribourg collection is unique in its transfer of the old quillwork pattern to silk-thread embroidery, with only a few glass beads used in the decoration of the ankle flaps.

Because of the bad state of conservation of this pair, only a detail of the decorated portions is shown in the accompanying illustration.

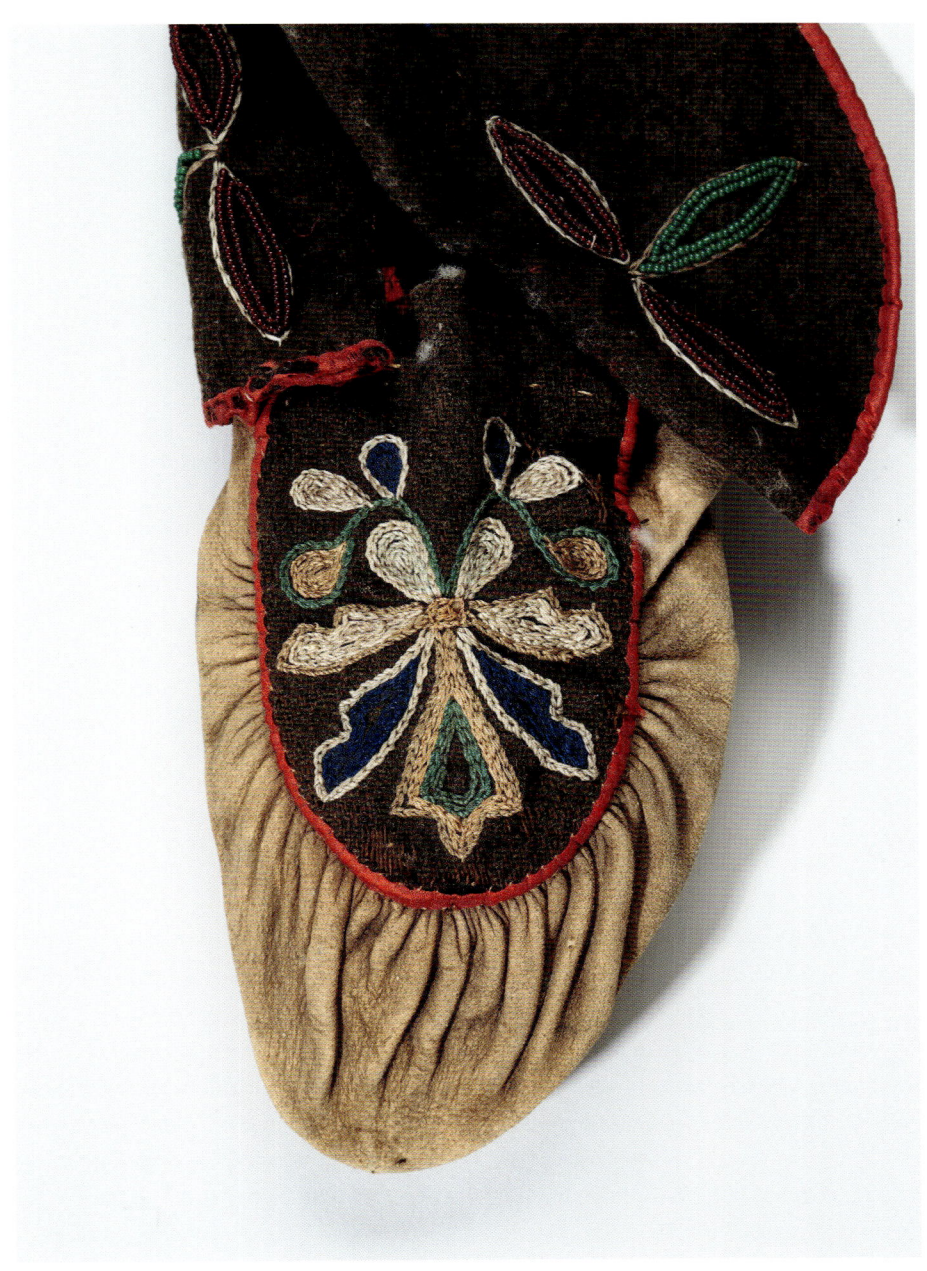

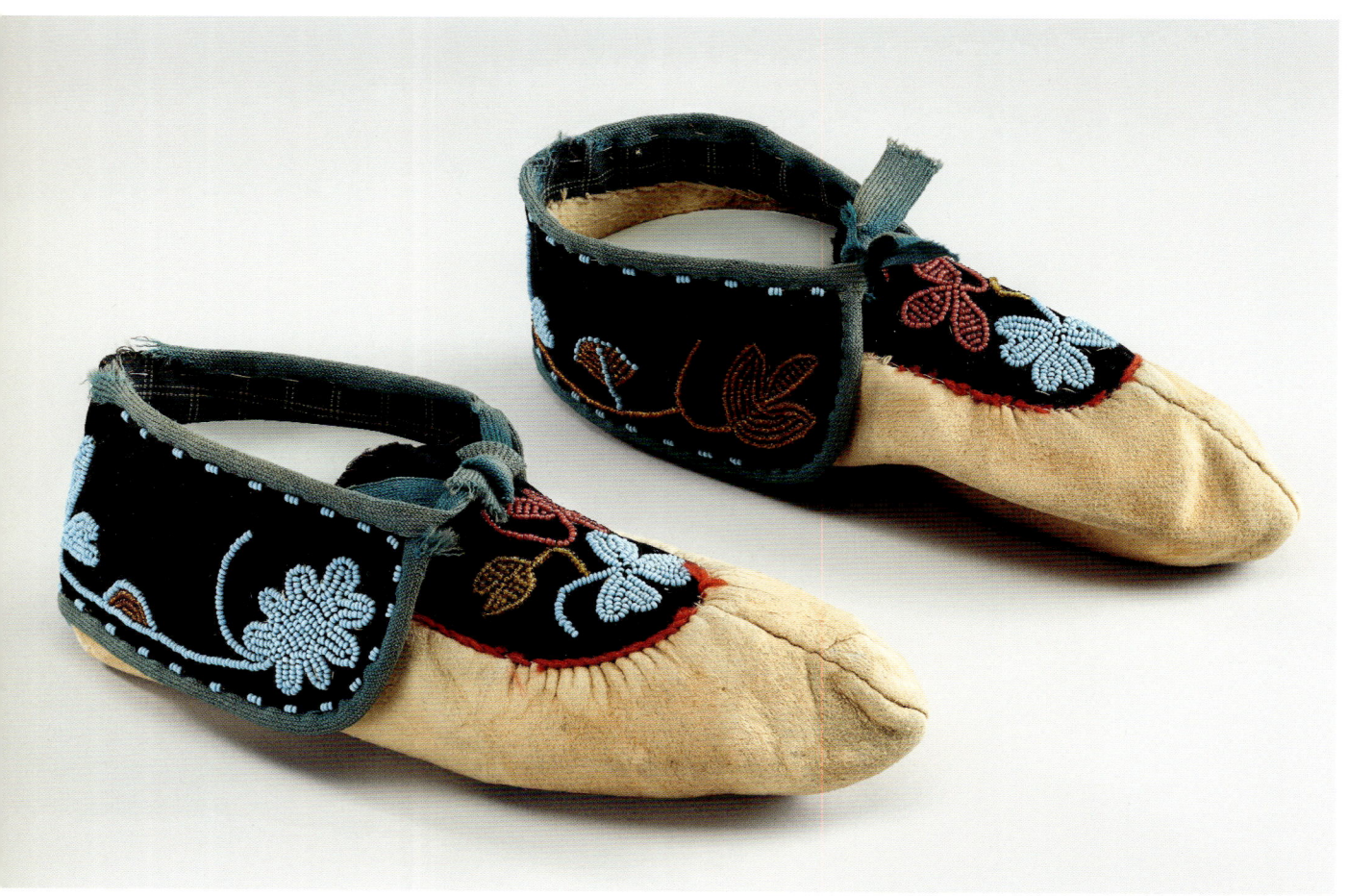

Moccasins
Buckskin, black velvet, glass beads, wool, cloth ribbon, cotton yarn
L 23 cm, W 9.7 cm, H 7.5 cm
Cat.no. 2004 (Catalogue raisonné no. [31])

The 1940 catalogue entry merely refers to these moccasins as from Wisconsin and not specifically from the Menominees.

In addition to the changes in moccasin decoration, Menominee women began at about the same time to add another moccasin pattern to their repertoire. This second type, perhaps inspired by Chippewa examples (Skinner 1921: 117–118), had a T-shaped heel seam and a straight center toe seam in front of the apron as in the case of this pair. As far as beadwork technique ("spot stitch") was concerned, the Menominees preferred to outline design elements with a line of preferably white or other beads contrasting with the color of the filling, which was made up of lines running parallel to the outline (as in the earlier porcupine quill linework; see p. 78). Because this was also common among the Chippewas, it is sometimes designated the "northern" variety. In Menominee beadwork, however, one occasionally finds a combination of the "northern" and "southern" style of beading, in which filling ran at right angles to the outline, as in the example shown here.

This pair lacks the color contrast between outline and filling typical for Menominee work and is also comparatively simple in its design. It is possible that these moccasins were made for a non-Native market. (For a comparable Menominee pair, see National Museum of the American Indian, cat.no. 16/9151, William C. Barnard coll.).

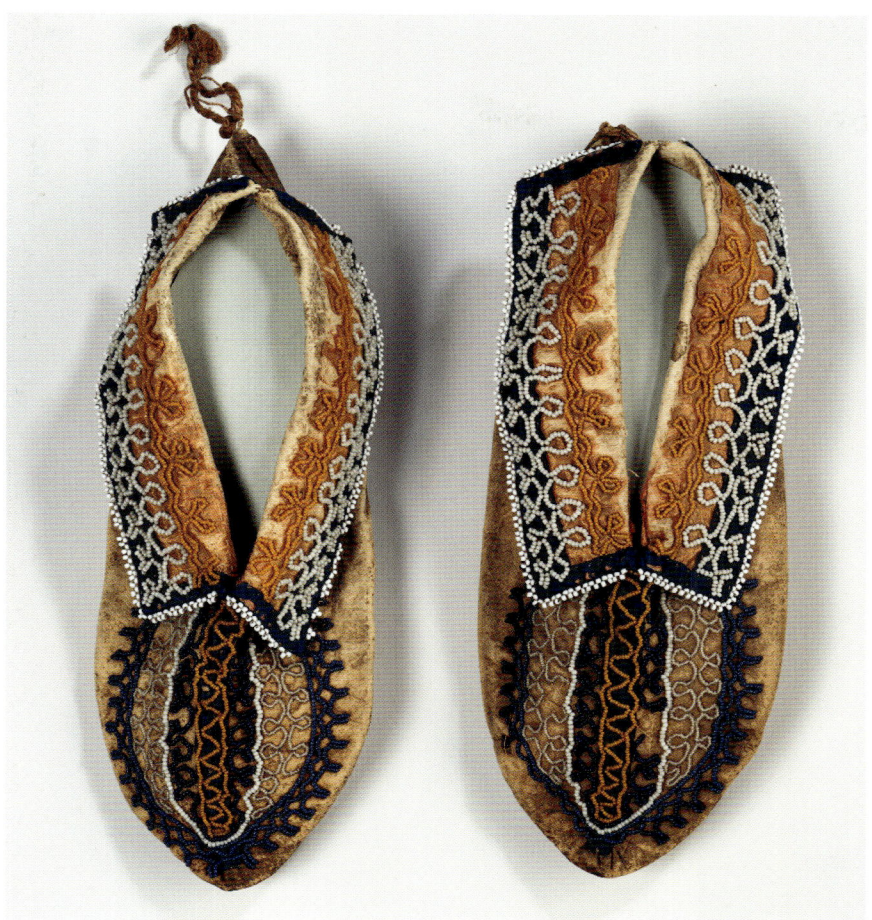

Moccasins

Buckskin, glass beads, silk and cloth ribbons, cotton yarn
L 24 cm, W 10.5 cm
Cat.no. 2006 (Catalogue raisonné no. [32])

Identified by a label attached to the object as "moc-casins of the wife of a pagan Indian chief," the style of this pair fits the time period of Gachet's collection and a possible provenance from Wisconsin but makes a Menominee origin unlikely.

The cut of the moccasins with a straight toe seam covered with apron-shaped bead appliqué and the beadwork patterns seem to be of Iroquois work and may point to an origin among the Oneida, who in the 1820s and 1830s had moved to Wisconsin. The use of silk ribbons as a backing of the beadwork on the ankle flaps and over the toe seam may reflect an inspiration derived from the popularity of ribbonwork among the

Menominees (who, however, did not combine bead-work and ribbonwork).

The identification of the maker as the wife of a "pagan" chief could indicate that she was an Oneida (who, including their chiefs, were mostly Christians) married to a Menominee. Gachet occasionally refers to intertribal marriages and more frequently to the conflicts arising out of marriages between Christians and adher-ents of the traditional religion, which the Catholic Church discouraged but was unable to prevent (Gachet 1860: 139–140, 235–237, 241, 248–249, 287).

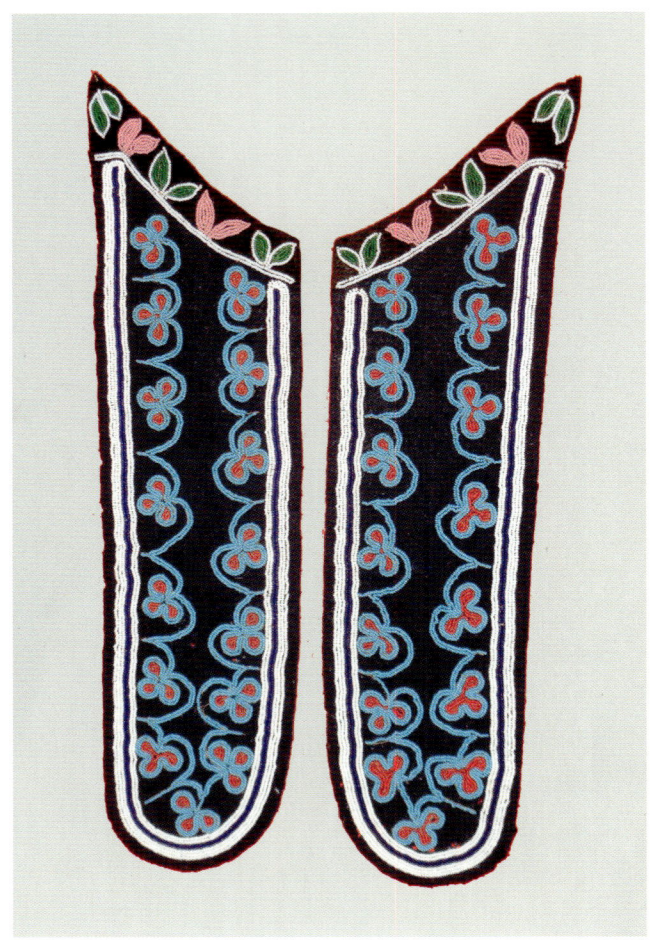

Pair of lapels for a coat
Cloth, glass beads, yarn
L 52 cm, W 13.5–14 cm (each)
Cat.no. 2045ab (Catalogue raisonné no. [33])

In the early days of the fur trade, Indian trading captains were courted by the fur traders with gifts of military-style coats, which sparked the development of a whole new genre of indigenous men's costumes. Especially coats made of cloth were often richly decorated with floral beadwork either directly sewn to the coat or to separate collars, bibs, or lapels attached to the garment. Lavishly beaded coats of this kind are often primarily associated with the Métis people of Canada, who also served as traders and cultural brokers among the indigenous peoples south of the U.S. border, or with equally culturally hybrid "Indian scouts." In the twentieth century beaded

lapels also appear as part of Native American dance outfits, including those of the Menominees (see, e.g., Marquette University Library, Special Collections, Franciscan Records, Photographs, Box 1, Folder 22).

Coats with beaded lapels are rather rare in collections (see, e.g., one presumably worn by the Métis leader Louis Riel in the Canadian Museum of History, cat.no. E-111, or a scout jacket in the Minnesota Historical Society, cat.no. 6585.1). The beadwork on the comparatively simple but elegant lapels in Fribourg is done in the "northern" variety of bead appliqué (see p. 80), although stylistically it is far from typical.

If they were collected by Gachet, he could have acquired them in the course of his many contacts with the Métis on the reservation (Gachet 1890: 122, 129, 133, 167, 243) or from Indians associated with them.

CATALOGUE RAISONNÉ

This catalogue begins with the items for which Gachet's original numbers are documented or can be reconstructed, followed by those for which unnumbered label copies are available. The final numbers in square brackets refer to other objects likely to have been collected by Gachet.

Abbreviations

LO: Label on object
LC: Typescript copies of the original labels
1940 Inv.: "Maschinschriftliche Bestandsaufnahme der Ethnologischen Sammlung des Cantons Fribourg 1940" ["Typewritten Inventory of the Ethnological Collection of the Canton Fribourg 1940," lists contents of crates with Roman numbers)
CC: Card catalogue, Musée d'Ethnographie, Université de Fribourg, undated (1980s)
Cat.no.:   Catalogue number assigned to the objects between 1986 and 1989
           Previous catalogue numbers on "old label" (square, white, ink), "new label" (round, white, ball pen), "recent label" (round, white, pencil)
D: Description: materials and dimensions
           (all measurements in cm: L=length, W=width, H=height, D=diameter);
           additional notes

01. Pipestem (p. 56)
LO: [1. Cal]umet des Ménomonies. (Don du R^d P. Antoine Marie cap.)
LC: Calumet des Folles-Avoines ou Ménomonies.
1940 Inv.: XIII.9 (1) Pfeifenrohr.
CC: —
Cat.no.: 2054, recent label 41
D: Wood with hot tool marks and cutout decorations, red

and green pigments
L 90.5, W 7.0, H 1.5

02. Pipestem (p. 55)
LO: [only small fragment of label remains]
LC: Calumet neuf en dards de porc-épic et en crin, confectionné pour le donateur par une Indienne.
1940 Inv.: XIII.7 (2) Pfeifenrohr mit Bast überwunden, vielfärbig.
CC: —
Cat.no.: 2055
D: Wood with hot tool marks; horsehair, porcupine quills (white, orange, blue), red and green silk ribbons (missing on upper side); backed with white cotton cloth on one side (apparently for conservation)
L 86.8, W 4.8–5.2, H 1.4

03. Pipestem (p. 57)
LO: 3. Tuyau de pipe des Ménomonies. (Don du R^d P. Ant. Marie)
LC: Tuyau de pipe des Ménomonies.
1940 Inv.: VIII.1 (3) Pfeifenrohr, flach, leicht verziert.
CC: —
Cat.no.: 2056
D: Wood with hot tool marks
L 84.2, W 2.3–3.3, H 1.8

04. Pipestem (cp. Fig. 52)
LO: —
LC: Tuyau de pipe d'un Indien Otchipway, homme du Wabanon ou de l'Est.
1940 Inv.: XIII.10 (4) Pfeifenrohr einer Indianerpfeife.
CC: Pfeifenrohr, L 101 cm, aus Holz, ... mit einem Vogelschnabel besetzt. Spuren einer roten Fassonierung. Messingbenägelung. ... Ojibway.

Cat.no.: —
D: Pipestem of wood, with bird skins, (silk?) ribbons, and brass tacks; object "repatriated" in 1980s (Feest 1995: 38–39).

05. Tobacco bag of muskrat skin (cp. Fig. 54)
LO: —
LC: Poche à tabac en peau de rat musqué, avec quelques restes de tabac indien appelé Pascharvan.
1940 Inv.: —
CC: —
Cat.no.: —
D: Object missing
Another tobacco bag is shown in one of Gachet's drawings (see p. 61, Fig. 54): "Shikak-Pétzénémawon ['skunk tobacco bag']. Tobacco bag of the skin of a skunk (Mephitis Americana)." According to Skinner (1921: 365–366) such bags (pe'tcînamauan) were rarely decorated and were distinguished from the otherwise similar medicine bags by the absence of tufts of dyed down thrust through the animal's nose.
The generic term "Pétzénémawon" is used by Gachet to refer to fingerwoven tobacco bags (see p. 40, Fig. 35).
The designation "Pascharvan" recorded by Gachet for tobacco actually refers to apä'sawan, the crude frame of saplings and basswood bark on which native tobacco substitutes were dried over a fire (Skinner 1921: 359).

06. Kinnikinnick
LO: —
LC: —
1940 Inv.: VIII.47   (11) Chinesischer Tabak.
CC: —
Cat.no.: —
D: Object missing
"The kini-ki[ni]k is the tobacco of our Indians and comes from the second bark of a certain shrub. Mixed with tobacco, it has a very good taste. ... Instead of kini-ki[ni]k our Indians also use the round leaf of a creeping plant, which they call sakakami" (Gachet 1890: 149, 194, 270). Hoffman (1896: 249–250) and Skinner (1921: 358–359) identify the sources of kinnikinnick as red osier (willow) bark and sumac leaves.

07. Pipe bowl (cp. Fig. 52)
LO: —
LC: Tête de pipe, ou calumet de la paix, en grand faveur parmi les Indiens, qui ne s'en défont que poussés par une extrême nécessité.
1940 Inv.: VIII.25   (7) Kopf einer Indianer Friedenspfeife, roter Ton.
CC: Kopf einer Friedenspfeife, Catlinit, Pfeifenfuss mit Kamm.
Cat.no.: —
D: Pipe bowl of catlinite; object missing.
The pipe bowl may have been "repatriated" together with the pipestem no. 04 (cp. Feest 1995: 38–39).

08.   Case for clay pipe (p. 58)
LO: 8. Etui de pipe indien. (Don du P. Ant. Marie)
LC: Etui de pipe indien.
1940 Inv.: VIII.24   Pfeifenetui aus Holz. Indien.
CC: Pfeifenetui.
Cat.no.: 2040
D: Wood, white cotton string, iron nail beaten to form a nut
L 27.7, H 7.2

09.   Ball-headed club (p. 59; cp. Fig. 54)
LO: [...] Folles Avoines [...] (Don du R. P. Antoine Marie)
LC: Oshko ou casse-tête d'un guerrier des Ménomonies. Les croix marquées sur le manche indiquent le nombre des ennemis tués par le propriétaire.
1940 Inv.: VIII.15   (9) Keule aus Holz (Folles-Avoines).
CC: —
Cat.no.: 2041
D: Wood with hot tool marks and engravings; traces of blue paint on ball and adjoining parts of shaft
L 52, D (ball) 5.2–6.5
"Oshko" in the transcription of the original label may have been miscopied from what was still legible of "Pakwokosh," the Menominee designation recorded by Gachet (cp. p. 59).

10.   Lacrosse stick and ball (p. 60; cp. Fig. 54)
LO: [10.] Pakath, jeu de balle indien. (Don du R. P. Ant. Marie)
LC: Pakath, crosse indienne avec sa balle servant au jeu national de ce nom, objets confectionnés par un chef chrétien.
1940 Inv.: VIII.4   Pakath, indisches Nationalspiel, Holzstab, wie Bischofsstab, mit Lederball.
CC: Ballspiel (Wurfstab und Ball)
Cat.nos.: 2043 (lacrosse stick), 2039 (leather ball)
D: Lacrosse stick and ball; wood, leather, sinew
L 65.7, D (ring) 7.4; D (ball) 4.8

11.   Birchbark fan
LO: —
LC: —
1940 Inv.: II.9   (6) Fächer des Stammeshäuptlings der Oshkosh [sic].
CC: Geisterwimpel, L 38 cm, zwei nach unten zusammenlaufende Birkenrindenteile mit blauem Stoffband zusammengenäht.
Cat.no.: —
D: Birchbark fan with porcupine quill decoration and blue ribbon edging; object missing. Another one sent to the Bishop of Lausanne and Geneva (p. 38) also missing.
The fan was still in existence in 1972, when it was exhibited as a "ghost banner, of birchbark, simple band decoration, with griffin feathers" (Schloss Heidegg 1972: 16).
Two such fans with hourglass-shaped handles made

around 1840 by the Menominee wife of the trader Augustin Grignon are in the Neville Public Museum, Green Bay, WI (cat.nos. L2800–2801). A very similar fan from the same period was also illustrated by Castelnau (see p. 45, Fig. 42, no. 6). Another fan collected in Wisconsin before 1851 is in the National Museum of Denmark (cat.no. E.Hc 220, M. L. Eylardi coll.).

The tapering handle of a birchbark fan depicted by Gachet in front of his portrait of a Catholic Menominee woman (p. 52, Fig. 51) corresponds more closely to the description given on the catalog card.

12. Lidded birchbark box (pp. 74–75; cp. Fig. 57)
LO: —
LC: Boîte en écorce, d'une femme indienne.
1940 Inv.: VIII.13 Rindenkörbchen mit Bast bestickt
CC: —
Cat.no.: 2008, old label N.31, new label 74
D: Lidded basket with handle; birchbark, dyed porcupine quills (white, yellow, red, blue, black), black velvet, red silk ribbons (now faded); lined with 1860 newspaper (*Advocate and Guardian*)
16.5 × 12.5 × 16.7, base 13.5 × 14.5

13. Miniature birchbark canoe (p. 65)
LO: 13. Canot d'écorce en miniature, fait par un vieil Indien (Don du R. P. Ant. Marie)
LC: Canot d'écorce en miniature, fait par un vieil Indien.
1940 Inv.: VIII.18 (13) Modell eines Rindenbootes der Indianer. Nordamerika.
CC: —
Cat.no.: 2066, old label N.17, new label 43, recent label 8
D: Birchbark, wood, spruce roots, red and green pigments, resin
L 64.2, W 17.6, H (bow/stern) 16.8–17.7, (center) 9.3–9.8
Given to Gachet by the maker in August 1860 (Gachet 1890: 245)

14. Miniature dugout canoe (pp. 66–67)
LO: 14. Canot de bois en min., servant aux Indiens pour la pêche et la chasse. (D. du R. P. Ant. Marie.)
LC: Canot de bois en miniature fait par un chef indien chrétien; représentation parfaite des pirogues indiennes d'une seule pièce de 15 à 20 pieds, servant aux Indiens pour la pêche et la chasse.
1940 Inv.: V.3 (14) Modell eines Holzbootes der Indianer für Fischerei und Jagd.
CC: —
Cat.no.: 2065, new label 30, recent label 11
D: Wood, red pigment (on upper edge, red dots on bow and stern)
L 40, W 8, H (bow/stern) 6.9–7.4, (center) 4.1
Given to Gachet by the maker in August 1860 together with the model of the birchbark canoe (Gachet 1890: 245)

15. Birchbark wrapper for maple sugar (p. 69)
LO: 15. Échantillon de sucre d'érable indien. (Don du R. P. Ant. Marie)
LC: Échantillon de sucre d'érable indien, appelé "de la tire" parce que les Indiens le confectionnent en tirant la pâte a deux mains.
1940 Inv.: V.1 (15) Muster von Ahornzucker der Indianer.
CC: —
Cat.no.: 2031 (maple sugar), 2076 (birchbark wrapper), old label N.3
D: The birchbark wrapper apparently once contained the samples of "twisted" maple sugar today stored together with other samples in two glass jars (cp. no. 19b below)
21.5 × 12 (folded)

16. Engraved board (p. 63)
LO: 16. Totem, armoiries indiennes, trouvé dans une cimetière païen (Indes). (Don du P. Ant. Marie)
LC: —
1940 Inv.: 1.26 (16) Totem. Eine Art Indianerwappen aus einem Grabe.
CC: —
Cat.no.: 2036, new label 37
D: Wood, red and green pigments; slightly convex and grooved surface, traces of sawing at the narrow sides; surface of wood weathered as if by exposure to moisture. Square, blackened groove on backside, probably for attachment
L 45, W 13.5, H 1.5–2

17. Two pincushions (p. 73)
LO: (a) 17. Ouvrages des femmes indiennes (D. du. P. A.-Marie)
(b) —
LC: Ouvrages des femmes indiennes.
1940 Inv.: —
CC: —
Cat.nos.: (a) 2013, new label 55
(b) 2014, new label (a) 55
D: (a) Round; birchbark, porcupine quills (white, yellow, red, blue, black), green silk ribbon; filling of old pieces of leather, printed cotton fabrics, fragments of a woolen fabric, unbleached cotton. Poor state of conservation
D 9
(b) Diamond-shaped pincushion; birchbark, porcupine quills (white, yellow, red, blue), translucent yellow glass beads, dark brown cloth, cotton filling. Poor state of conservation
L 8.2, W 7.4, H 2.5–3.4

18. Two mococks containing maple sugar (p. 71)
LO: 2 Boîtes de sucre d'érable, avec dessins en dards de porc-épic et bouleau. Ouvrage d'indiennes. (Don du Rd P. Ant. Marie)
LC: Boîte a sucre d'érable fabriqué par des Indiennes.
1940 Inv.: VIII.29 (18) Rindentüte für Zucker. Indianerarbeit.
CC: —

Cat.nos.: (a) 2010, old label N.9, new label 48
(b) 2009, old label (a) N.5, new label 59
D: (a) Mocock containing maple sugar; birchbark, porcupine quills (white, yellow, red, blue, black); sewn with yarn. Poor state of conservation
H 6.5, top 8.9 × 5.7, base 9 × 5.2
(b) Mocock containing maple sugar; birchbark, porcupine quills (white, yellow, red, blue, black); sewn with yarn. Poor state of conservation
H 5.8, top 8.5 × 5.9, base 8 × 4.7

19. Two glass jars with maple sugar candies (pp. 69–70)
LO: (a) 19. Sucre d'érable fabriqué par les Indiennes donné en 1860 par le R. P. Ant. Marie (Gachet), capucin, missionaire chez les Ménomonies, au nord du Wisconsin (Amérique)
(b) 19. Échantillon de sucre d'érable fabriqué par des Indiennes (D. du R. P. Ant. Marie)
(both labels on both jars)
LC: Échantillons de sucre d'érable fabriqués par des Indiennes.
1940 Inv.: II.10 (19) Muster von Baumzucker von den Indianern hergestellt.
Cat.nos.: (a) 2030, new label (a) 39, recent label 60
(b) 2031, new label 38, recent label 61
D: (a) 9 pieces and fragments in cylindrical glass jar
Two heart-shaped pieces: L 7.1 and 6.7
Broken leaf-shaped piece
Round with cross, 4 dots: D 5.6
Round with wavy edge: D 6.0
Fragment of veined leaf: W 7.3
Elongated leaf-shaped (two fragments): L 9.5
Round with cross (fragment)
(b) 5 pieces in cylindrical glass jar
Twisted stick (2 parts): L 15.6
Face: L 7.1, W 5.8
Veined leaf: L 7.7
Round with quadrilateral pattern: D 5.9
Round with wavy edge: D 7.7

20. Thin sheets of birchbark (p. 64)
LO: 20. Cahier en feuilles d'écorce de bouleau. (Don du R. P. Ant. Marie)
LC: Cahier en feuilles d'écorce de bouleau.
1940 Inv.: II.11 (20) Blätter zum Beschreiben aus Birkenrinde.
CC: —
Cat.no.: 2077
D: Birchbark
14.5 × 8.4

21. Jacklight for miniature canoe (pp. 66–67)
LO: 21. Appareil de chasse s'adaptant au canot No. 14. (Don du R. P. Antoine-Marie)
LC: Appareil de chasse s'adaptant au canot.
1940 Inv.: VIII.19 Modell einer Jagdvorrichtung zum Bootsmodell in Kiste V.

CC: —
Cat.no.: 2064, old label N.14, new label 4
D: Wood
L 17.2, W 3.6

22. Spoon (p. 72)
LO: —
LC: Cuiller en bois de fabrication indienne.
1940 Inv.: —
CC: —
Cat.no.: 2037, new label 17
D: Wood with cutout decoration and hot tool marks on upper lateral edges
L 11.8, W (bowl) 6.2

23. Spearhead (p. 62)
LO: —
LC: Bout de lance en bronze des anciens Indiens
1940 Inv.: —
CC: —
Cat.no.: 2062
D: Copper, patined, half socket on base
L 13.6, W 2.3

24. Spearheads, arrowheads, and knives of flint
LO: —
LC: Lances, flèches et couteaux en silex des anciens Indiens
1940 Inv.: —
CC: —
Cat.no.: —
D: Objects missing
In June 1860 Gachet (1890: 243) noted in his diary the gift of "a flint arrowhead and fragments of an ancient Indian vase and pipe bowl" found "in the vicinity" by the donor, a member of a local Métis family.

25. Fragments of an ancient vessel
LO: —
LC: Fragments d'une pièce de vaisselle des anciens Indiens
1940 Inv.: —
CC: —
Cat.no.: —
D: Object missing
See the comment on number 24.

26. Fragment of catlinite
LO: —
LC: Fragment de la pierre sacrée dont les Indiens confectionnent le calumet de la paix
1940 Inv.: —
CC: —
Cat.no.: —
D: Object missing
The text of the label is based on a note in Gachet's diary: "I will speak in due course of the sacred rock, a kind of red stone from which the Indians manufacture their pipes of peace and war. This stone is found in

Minnesota; it is to the savages what the Kaaba is to Muslims" (Gachet 1890: 133).

27. Medicine bags
LO: —
LC: Sachets à amulettes des Indiens
1940 Inv.: —
CC: —
Cat.no.: —
D: Objects missing
The French term "sachet" is used in Gachet's diary both for small bags containing amulets and worn suspended from the neck and for the larger animal skin pouches. On several occasions he inspected the contents of the numerous medicine bags of otter, weasel, or skunk skin delivered to him by neophytes, who had formerly been members of the Medicine Society, before consigning them to the flames (Gachet 1890: 284–285). Elsewhere, however, he takes a more favorable view of these bags "carried by those whose mission it is to heal and not to harm their fellows, as witches do." The now missing objects may have included "the medicine bag of a woman that I had baptized," containing "the skin of a hawk with its crooked beak and sharp talons" (Gachet 1890: 178) and/or the smaller bags, which were twined of vegetable fibers and by Skinner's time had been superseded by small bags of woven beadwork (Skinner 1921: pls. LXVII–LXXIII).

28. European officer's emblem
LO: —
LC: Ancienne décoration d'un officier européen, ayant servi à l'enharnachement de pony d'un Indien.
1940 Inv.: —
CC: —
Cat.no.: —
D: Object missing
In 1859 Gachet (1890: 172) met a Menominee who "appeared to be a dandy of the tribe; he had his hair plaited in a single braid and wore an officer's collar, probably a souvenir of Black Hawk's War" (in which Menominee warriors participated on the American side). While this is obviously not the object in Gachet's collection, it illustrates the Menominee use of foreign and presumably powerful objects for decorative purposes.

29. Mittens (pp. 76–77; cp. Fig. 58)
LO: —
LC: Paire de gants des Indiens Ménomonie.
1940 Inv.: V.4 (11) Lederhandschuhe der Indianer mit Perlen bestickt.
CC: —
Cat.no.: 2001, new label 58
D: Buckskin; translucent and opaque glass beads (clear, yellow, pink, dark red, blue, dark blue, green), black silk ribbon, yarn
L 25.5, W 12.5

[30.] Moccasins (pp. 78–79; cp. Fig. 59)
LO: —
LC: —
1940 Inv.: V.28 Mocassin aus Leder mit Stickerei, Nordamerika.
CC: —
Cat.no.: 2005
D: Buckskin, apron, T-heel seam; brownish, worn cloth lined with strong cotton fabric; silk thread (white, yellow, blue, green), glass beads (red and green) on flap, red silk ribbon, remains of green and yellow silk ribbons, yarn
L 25.5, W 10, H 9.5
The source for these moccasins and/or those listed below could be the gifts by Gachet to Comte de Diesbach and Madame la Comtesse Fegely Maillardoz (see p. 38).

[31.] Moccasins (p. 80)
LO: —
LC: —
1940 Inv.: V.23 Moccasins der Indianer von Wisconsin, Leder und Samt mit bunter Perlenstickerei.
CC: —
Cat.no.: 2004, new label 51
D: Buckskin, apron with straight toe seam, T-heel seam; black velvet, checkered cotton cloth lining; glass beads (light blue, red, dark yellow, red wool, blue ribbon, yarn
L 23, W 9.7, H 7.5

[32.] Moccasins (p. 81)
LO: [not in Gachet's hand] Mocassins der Frau eines heidnischen Indianer H[äuptlings]
LC: —
1940 Inv.: III.2 Lederschuhe mit Perlenstickerei. Mocassins der Frau eines Indianerhäuptlings aus Chile.
CC: —
Cat.no.: 2006, new label 83
D: Buckskin, straight heel seam, straight toe seam; blue and light pink silk ribbon, glass beads (white, pearl, translucent, yellow, black), yarn
L 24, W 10.5, H 6.3

[33.] Pair of beaded lapels for a coat (p. 82)
LO: —
LC: —
1940 inv.: —
CC: —
Cat.no.: 2045ab
D: Blue cloth, glass beads (white, dark and light blue, green, pink, red)
L 52, W 13.5–14 (each)

BIBLIOGRAPHY

Alderson, Jo Bartels, and J. Michael Alderson
1974 *The Man Mazzuchelli.* Madison, WI: Wisconsin House.

Baraga, Friedrich
1837 *Geschichte, Character, Sitten und Gebräuche der nord-amerikanischen Indier.* Laibach: Joseph Blasnik.
1850 *A Theoretical and Practical Grammar of the Otchipwe Language.* Detroit, MI: Jabez Fox.
1853 *A Dictionary of the Otchipwe Language.* Cincinnati, OH: Jos. A. Hemann. [2nd ed.: Toronto 1878.]
1858 *Katolik anaimie-misinaigan wetawawissing.* Cincinnati, OH: Joseph A. Hemann.

Beck, David R. M.
2002 *Siege and Survival. History of the Menominee Indians, 1634–1856.* Lincoln, NE: University of Nebraska Press.

Berg, Dieter, and Leonhard Lehmann
2009 (eds.) *Franziskus-Quellen. Die Schriften des heiligen Franziskus, Lebensbeschreibungen, Chroniken und Zeugnisse über ihn und seinen Orden.* Kevelaer: Butzon & Bercker.

Berkhofer, Robert F., Jr.
1976 *Salvation and the Savage. An Analysis of Protestant Missions and American Indian Response, 1787–1862.* New York, NY: Atheneum.

Bieder, Robert E.
1995 *Native American Communities in Wisconsin, 1600–1960. A Study of Tradition and Change.* Madison, WI: University of Wisconsin Press.

Bittle, Celestine N.
1934–1935 Father Anthony Maria Gachet, O. M. Cap. Five Years in America. *Wisconsin Magazine of History* 18(1): 66–76, (2): 191–204, (3): 345–359.

Bloomfield, Leonard
1962 *The Menominee Language.* New Haven, CT: Yale University Press.

1975 *Menominee Lexicon.* Charles F. Hockett, ed. Milwaukee Public Museum Publications in Anthropology and History 3. Milwaukee, WI.

Bonduel, Florimond J.
1851 Letter to William Clarey, Lake Poygan, Wisconsin, 2 April 1851. United States National Archives, Washington, DC (OIA, Letters Received, Reel 321: 218–219).
1855 *Tableau comparatif entre la condition morale des tribus indiennes de l'état du Wisconsin.* Tournai: J. Casterman et fils.

Castelnau, Francis de
1842 *Vues et souvenirs de l'Amérique du Nord.* Paris: A. Bertrand.

Comaroff, John, and Jean Comaroff
1991 *Of Revelation and Revolution: Christianity, Colonialism and Consciousness in South Africa.* Chicago, IL: University of Chicago Press.

Culin, Stewart
1907 Games of the North American Indians. *Twenty-Fourth Annual Report of the Bureau of American Ethnology* (Washington, DC), 1–846.

Densmore, Frances
1932 *Menominee Music.* Bulletin of the Bureau of American Ethnology 102. Washington, DC.

Direction de l'Instruction Publique
1860 Letter to the Guardian of the Capuchin Order, Fribourg, 28 November 1860. Archives, Capuchin Friary, Fribourg.
1868 Letter to Antoine Marie Gachet, Fribourg, 22 February 1868. Archives, Capuchin Friary, Fribourg.

Esser, Kajetan
1978 (ed.) *Opuscula Sancti Patris Francisci Assisiensis.* Roma: Grottaferrata.

Favre, Blaise
1954a La tribu indienne des Menomonies et l'évolution

de la religion d'après le P. A. M. Gachet et A. B. Skinner. Unpublished Lic. thesis, University of Fribourg.

1954b La grammaire de la langue ménomonie du P. Antoine Marie Gachet. *Anthropos* 49: 1094–1100.

Feder, Norman

1964 *Art of the Eastern Plains Indians. The Nathan Sturges Jarvis Collection.* Brooklyn, NY: The Brooklyn Museum.

1965 *American Indian Art before 1850.* Denver Art Museum Summer Quarterly 1965. Denver, CO.

Feest, Christian F.

1968 *Indianer Nordamerikas.* Wien: Museum für Völkerkunde.

1995 "Repatriation": A European View on the Question of Restitution of Native American Artifacts. *European Review of Native American Studies* 9(2): 33–42.

1998 The Native American Collection of Friderik Baraga: Comparative and Contextual Aspects. *Etnolog* 8(59): 285–312.

2002 Knife Cases from Northeastern North America. In: I. Goddard and W. L. Merrill (eds.), *Anthropology, History, and American Indians: Essays in Honor of William Curtis Sturtevant* (Smithsonian Contributions to Anthropology 44, Washington, DC 2002), 263–278.

2008a (ed.) *Indianer. Ureinwohner Nordamerikas.* Schallaburg: Schallaburg Kulturbetriebsges.m.b.H.

2008b Moravians and the Development of the Genre of Ethnography. In: A. Gregg Roeber (ed.), *Ethnographies and Exchanges* (University Park, PA 2008: Penn State Press), 19–30.

Feest, Christian F., and Sylvia S. Kasprycki

1993 *Über/Lebenskunst nordamerikanischer Indianer.* Wien: Museum für Völkerkunde.

1999 *Peoples of the Twilight: European Views of Native Minnesota, 1823 to 1862.* Afton, MN: Afton Historical Society Press.

2001 Comparative Evidence, Critical Reasoning, and the Identification of Styles: A (Knife)Case in Point. In: Christian F. Feest (ed.), *Studies in American Indian Art. A Memorial Tribute to Norman Feder* (ERNAS Monographs 2; Altenstadt), 187–204.

Flint Institute of Arts

1973 *Art of the Great Lakes Indians.* Flint, MI: Flint Institute of Arts.

Francis of Assisi

1999 *Early Documents, Volume I: The Saint.* New York, NY: New City Press.

Gachet, Antoine Marie

1858 Letter to Bishop Anastasius Hartmann, Calvary, Wisconsin, 21 December 1858. (Copy.) Archives, Province of St. Joseph of the Capuchin Order, Detroit, MI.

1859 Letter to Bishop Martin Henni, Keshena, Wisconsin, 2 August 1859. (Copy.) Archives, Province of St. Joseph of the Capuchin Order, Detroit, MI.

1861 Letter to Bishop Martin Henni, Keshena, Wisconsin, 4 April 1861. (Copy.) Archives, Province of St. Joseph of the Capuchin Order, Detroit, MI.

1862a Menominee Catechisme. Provinzarchiv der Schweizer Kapuziner, Luzern (Box 2245.5, Map "Opera").

1862b Liste des Indiens Folles-Avoines payens /Wisconsin, Amerique Sept./ que j'ai baptisés du 1 Juin 1859 au 14 Mars 1862. Manuscript. Provinzarchiv der Schweizer Kapuziner, Luzern (Box 2245.5).

1876 *Vie de Mgr. Anastase Hartmann de l'ordre des F.F. Mineurs Capucins.* Fribourg: Impr. de St. Paul.

1890 *Cinq ans en Amérique. Journal d'un missionnaire.* Fribourg: Imprimerie Catholique Suisse.

1954 *Grammaire de la langue Ménomonie.* Micro-Bibliotheca Anthropos 21. Fribourg.

s.a. [Menominee Grammar]. Manuscript, Provinzmuseum der Schweizer Kapuziner, Sursee (cat.no. 357).

Golob, France

1997 *Misijonarji, darovalci indijanskih predmetov: zbirka Slovenskega etnografeskega muzeja.* Knjižnica Slovenskega etnografeskega muzeja 5. Ljubljana.

Graham, Stephen

1983 (ed.) *Ottawa Quillwork on Birchbark.* Harbor Springs, MI: Harbor Springs Historical Commission.

1984 (ed.) *Beadwork and Textiles of the Ottawa.* Harbor Springs, MI: Harbor Springs Historical Commission.

Grangier, Louis

1880–1881 Notice historique sur le Musée cantonal de Fribourg. *Bulletin de la Société Fribourgeoise des Sciences Naturelles* 2: 50–96.

1891 Nécrologie. *Nouvelles Étrennes Fribourgeoises, Almanach des Villes et des Campagnes, publiée sous le patronage de la Société Économique et d'utilité publique de Fribourg* 25: 77–79.

Griffin, James B.

1961 (ed.) *Lake Superior Copper and the Indians.* University of Michigan, Museum of Anthropology, Anthropological Papers 17. Ann Arbor, MI.

Hallowell, A. Irving

1960 The Beginnings of Anthropology in America. In: Frederica de Laguna (ed.), *Selected Papers from the American Anthropologist 1880–1920* (Washington, DC: American Anthropological Association), 1–90.

Harper, J. Russell

1971 *Paul Kane's Frontier. (Including Wanderings of an Artist among the Indians of North America by Paul Kane.)* Austin, TX: University of Texas Press.

Harrison, Julia, et al.

1987 *The Spirit Sings. Artistic Traditions of Canada's First Peoples. A Catalogue of the Exhibition.* Toronto, ON: McClelland and Stewart.

Hartmann, Anastasius

2003 *Autobiographie des Anastasius Hartmann (1803–1866), des Schweizer Kapuziners, Titularbischofs von Derbe und apostolischen Vikars von Patna in Indien.* Helvetia Franciscana, Beiheft 4. Luzern.

Hoffman, Walter J.

1896 *The Menomini Indians.* Fourteenth Annual Report of the Bureau of American Ethnology. Washington, DC: Government Printing Office.

Kane, Paul

1859   *Wanderings of an Artist among the Indians of North America*. London: Longman, Brown, Green.

Kasprycki, Sylvia S.

1990a Image and Imagination. Menominee Portraits, 1825–1860. *Archiv für Völkerkunde* 44: 65–131.

1990b "A Lover of All Knowledge": Edwin James and Menominee Ethnography. *European Review of Native American Studies* 4(1): 1–9.

1994   Sirens, Tapirs, and Egyptian Totems: Toward an Interpretation of Menominee Religious Iconography. *Archiv für Völkerkunde* 48: 93–120.

1996   Matters of Faith: Notes on Missionaries and Material Culture. *European Review of Native American Studies* 10(2): 45–50.

1998   The Native American Collection of Friderik Baraga: The Missionary as Ethnographic Collector. *Etnolog* 8(59): 331–355.

2005   Gachet und wie er die Welt sah: Von Ethnologen, Missionaren und der Faszination der Dinge. In: Cora Bender, Christian Carstensen, Henry Kammler und Sylvia S. Kasprycki (eds.), *Ding – Bild – Wissen. Ergebnisse und Perspektiven amerikanistischer Ethnologie in Frankfurt am Main* (Studien zur Kulturkunde 124. Köln: Rüdiger Köppe), 15–38.

2006   *Die Dinge des Glaubens. Menominees und Missionare im kulturellen Dialog, 1830–1880*. Wien—Berlin: LIT.

2007   A Devout Collector: Johann Georg Schwarz and Early Nineteenth-Century Menominee Art. In: J. C. H. King and Christian F. Feest (eds.), *Three Centuries of Woodlands Indian Art* (Altenstadt: ZKF Publishers), 113–122.

2008   Mission: Das Seengebiet im 19. Jahrhundert. In: Christian Feest (ed.), *Indianer. Ureinwohner Nordamerikas* (Schallaburg: Schallaburg Kulturbetriebsges. m.b.H.), 67–85.

2015   Quilled Trapezoidal Pouches from the Western Great Lakes Region. *American Indian Art Magazine* 40(4): 48–63.

Keesing, Felix M.

1987   *The Menomini Indians of Wisconsin. A Study of Three Centuries of Cultural Contact and Change*. [1939] Madison, WI: University of Wisconsin Press.

King, J. C. H.

1977   *Smoking Pipes of the North American Indian*. London: British Museum Publications.

Kinietz, Vernon W.

1965   *The Indians of the Western Great Lakes, 1615–1760*. [1940] Ann Arbor, MI: University of Michigan Press.

Kohl, Johann Georg

1859   *Kitschi-Gami oder Erzählungen vom Obern See. Ein Beitrag zur Charakteristik der amerikanischen Indianer*. Bremen: C. Schünemann.

Krusche, Rolf

1981   *The Wabeno Cult as an Adversary of the Midewiwin*. In: Pieter Hovens (ed.), North American Indian Studies: European Contributions (Göttingen: Herodot), 77–98.

Kummer, Gertrude

1966   *Die Leopoldinen-Stiftung (1829–1914). Der älteste österreichische Missionsverein*. Wien: Wiener Dom-Verlag.

MA

1946, 1948 *Monumenta Anastasiana*, vol. IV (1857–1863), vol. V (1863–1866). Adelheim Jann, ed. Luzern: Curia Provinciae Helveticae Ordinis Min. Cap.

Marcoy, Paul

1875   *Travels in South America from the Pacific Ocean to the Atlantic Ocean*. 2 vols. London: Blackie.

Mason, Carol I.

1990   A Sweet Small Something: Maple Sugaring in the New World. In: James A. Clifton (ed.), *The Invented Indian* (New Brunswick, NJ: Transaction Publishers), 91–105.

Mazzuchelli, Samuele

1915   *Memoirs Historical and Edifying, of a Missionary Apostolic of the Order of St. Dominic Among Various Indian Tribes* [...]. Chicago, IL: W. F. Hall.

Merrill, William L.

1993   Conversion and Colonialism in Northern Mexico. The Tarahumara Response to the Jesuit Mission Program, 1601–1767. In Robert W. Hefner (ed.), *Conversion to Christianity. Historical and Anthropological Perspectives on a Great Transformation* (Berkeley, CA: University of Berkeley Press), 129–163.

Miner, Kenneth L.

1977   Review of *Menominee Lexicon* by Leonard Bloomfield. *International Journal of American Linguistics* 43(1): 66–73.

Morrison, Kenneth M.

1990   Baptism and Alliance: The Symbolic Mediations of Religious Syncretism. *Ethnohistory* 37(4): 416–437.

Ourada, Patricia K.

1979   *The Menominee Indians. A History*. Norman, OK: University of Oklahoma Press.

Penney, David W.

1992   *Art of the American Indian Frontier: The Chandler-Pohrt Collection*. Seattle, WA: University of Washington Press.

Phillips, Ruth B.

1998   *Trading Identities. The Souvenir in Native North American Art from the Northeast, 1700–1900*. Seattle, WA: University of Washington Press.

Pitzer, Martin

1854   *Verzeichniß der Gegenstände und Arbeiten eines Indianer-Stammes im nördlichsten Amerika nebst einer Charakteristik desselben*. München: J. G. Weiß'sche Universitäts-Buchdruckerei.

Rapaport, Ben

2014   The Clay Tobacco Pipe Case: An Ingenious European Tobacco Trifle. *Pipes & Tobacco Magazine* 18(4).

RCIA

1831–1883 U.S. Office of Indian Affairs, Report of the Commissioner of Indian Affairs to the Secretary of the Interior [varying titles]. Washington, DC: Government Printing Office.

Rese, Friedrich
1830   Letter to Joseph von Penkler, Cincinnati, OH, 20 January 1830. *Neue Theologische Zeitschrift* 3(1): 329–336.

Ritzenthaler, Robert E.
1979   *Prehistoric Indians of Wisconsin*. 2nd ed. Milwaukee Public Museum, Popular Science Handbook Series 4. Milwaukee, WI.

Rohrbacher, Peter
2012   Völkerkunde und Afrikanistik für den Papst: Österreichische Missionsexperten und der Vatikan, 1922– 1939. *Römische Historische Mitteilungen* 54: 583–610.

Rotzetter, Anton
1977   *Die Funktion der Franziskanischen Bewegung in der Kirche. Eine pastoraltheologische Interpretation der grundlegenden franziskanischen Texte*. Schwyz: Tau.
1982   Gott in der Verkündigung des hl. Franz. In: Ettore Covi (ed.), *L'esperienza di Dio in Francesco d'Assisi* (Dimensioni spirituali 3; Roma: Editrice Laurentianum), 40–76.
1984   Die missionarische Dimension des franziskanischen Charismas. *Franziskanische Studien* 66: 82–90.
1994   The Missionary Dimension of the Franciscan Charism. In: Anselm Moons and Flavian Walsh (eds.), *Mission in the Franciscan Tradition* (Spirit and Life 6; St. Bonaventure, NY: The Franciscan Institute), 47–57. [English translation of Rotzetter 1984.]
2008   Mystik und Mission bei Franz von Assisi. *Zeitschrift für Missionswissenschaft und für Religionswissenschaft* 92: 272–279.
2013   (ed.) *Franziskus – ein Name als Programm*. Kevelaer: Butzon & Bercker.

Ruegg, François
2015   (ed.) *Des collections sortent de l'oubli. Un trésor, une histoire*. Fribourg: Pro Ethnographi©a.

Schloss Heidegg
1972   *Auf großer Fahrt mit dem Häuptling Sitting Bull und dem Späher Buffalo Bill bei den Sioux-Indianern am Teufelssee*. S.l.

Schoolcraft, Henry Rowe
1821   *Narrative Journal of Travels through the Northwestern Regions of the United States [...]*. Albany, NY: E. & E. Hosford.

Schweizer, Christian
2007   Mount Calvary und Wesemlin Luzern. Die Anfänge der 150jährigen Präsenz der Kapuziner auf Mount Calvary in den USA und der Bezug zur Schweiz. *Helvetia Franciscana* 36: 94–109.

Skinner, Alanson B.
1911   The Menomini Game of Lacrosse. *American Museum Journal* 11(4): 139–141.
1913   Social Life and Ceremonial Bundles of the Menomini Indians. *Anthropological Papers of the American Museum of Natural History* 13: 1–165.

1915a   Associations and Ceremonies of the Menomini Indians. *Anthropological Papers of the American Museum of Natural History* 13: 167–215.
1915b   The Menomini Word "Häwätûk." *Journal of American Folklore* 28: 258–261.
1920   *Medicine Ceremony of the Menomini, Iowa, and Wahpeton Dakota, with Notes on the Ceremony among the Ponca, Bungi Ojibwa, and Potawatomi*. Indian Notes and Monographs 4. New York, NY.
1921   *Material Culture of the Menomini*. Indian Notes and Monographs 20. New York, NY.
1925   Songs of the Menomini Medicine Ceremony. *American Anthropologist*, n.s. 27(2): 290–314.

Skinner, Alanson B., and John V. Satterlee
1915   Folklore of the Menomini Indians. *Anthropological Papers of the American Museum of Natural History* 13: 217–546.

Smith, Alice E.
1973   *The History of Wisconsin. Vol. 1: From Exploration to Statehood*. Madison, WI: The State Historical Society of Wisconsin.

Smith, Huron H.
1923   *Ethnobotany of the Menomini Indians*. Bulletin of the Public City of Milwaukee 4, no. 1. Milwaukee, WI.

Spindler, George, and Louise Spindler
1984   *Dreamers with Power. The Menominee*. 2nd ed. Prospect Heights, IL: Waveland Press.

Staub, Friedrich, Ludwig Tobler, et al.
1881–2017   (eds.) *Schweizerisches Idiotikon. Wörterbuch der schweizerdeutschen Sprache*. 17 vols. Frauenfeld: Huber (after vol. 17 [2015ff]: Basel: Schwabe).

Trowbridge, Charles Christopher
1823   Traditions, Manner and Customs of the Mun-noá-min-nee Nation of Indians [...]. Ms., Burton Historical Collections, Detroit Public Library, Detroit, MI.

Vennum, Thomas, Jr.
1994   *American Indian Lacrosse. Little Brother of War*. Washington, DC: Smithsonian Institution Press.

Welsh, Peter H., et al.
1983   *Akicita. Early Plains and Woodlands Indian Art from the Collection of Alexander Acevedo*. Los Angeles, CA: The Southwest Museum.

White, Richard
1991   *The Middle Ground. Indians, Empires, and Republics in the Great Lakes Region, 1650–1815*. Cambridge: Cambridge University Press.

Whiteford, Andrew Hunter, and Nora Rogers
1994   Woven Mats of the Western Great Lakes. *American Indian Art Magazine* 19(4): 58–65.

Whitehead, Ruth Holmes
1982   *Micmac Quillwork*. Halifax, NS: The Nova Scotia Museum.

PICTURE CREDITS

Capuchin Friary, Fribourg (Switzerland)

Photographs: Francesco Ragusa
p. 8 (Fig. 2), p. 17 (Fig. 6), pp. 19–20 (Figs. 9–10), pp. 26–28 (Figs. 17–20) pp. 29–31 (Figs. 22–24), pp. 33–36 (Figs. 27–31), pp. 39–40 (Figs. 33–35), p. 41 (Fig. 38), p. 46 (Fig. 43), pp. 49–50 (Figs. 46–47), pp. 51–52 (Figs. 49–51), p. 54 (Fig. 52), p. 61 (Fig. 54), p. 66 (Fig. 55), p. 68 (Fig. 56), p. 75 (Fig. 57)

Photographs: Christian Feest/Sylvia Kasprycki
p. 6 (Fig. 1), p. 14 (Fig. 4), p. 17 (Fig. 5), p. 18 (Fig. 7), p. 24 (Fig. 14), p. 38 (Fig. 32), pp. 40–41 (Figs. 36–37), p. 42 (Fig. 40), p. 47 (Fig. 45), p. 76 (Fig. 58), p. 78 (Fig. 59)

Photograph: Ernest Lorson
p. 12 (Fig. 3)

Unknown photographer
p. 18 (Fig. 8)

Christian Feest, Altenstadt (Germany)
p. 23 (Fig. 12)

Milwaukee Public Museum, Milwaukee, WI (U.S.A.)
p. 25 (Figs. 15–16)

Oberösterreichisches Landesmuseum, Linz (Austria)
p. 58 (Fig. 53)

Pro Ethnographi©a, Fribourg (Switzerland)

Photographs: Francesco Ragusa
pp. 55–60, pp. 62–65, p. 67, pp. 69–70, p. 71 (left), p. 72, p. 73 (right), p. 74, p. 77, pp. 79–81

Photographs: Christian Feest/Sylvia Kasprycki
p. 71 (right), p. 73 (left)

Stark Museum of Art, Orange, TX (U.S.A.)
p. 31 (Fig. 24)

Wisconsin Historical Society, Madison, WI (U.S.A.)
p. 32 (Figs. 25–26)

INDEX